PSL'S PRACTICAL GUIDE TO
Railway Modelling

edited by Michael Andress

 PSL Patrick Stephens, Cambridge

First published 1981.

British Library Cataloguing in Publication Data

PSL's practical guide to railway modelling.—No. 1
  1. Railways—Models—Periodicals
  625.1'9   TF197

  ISBN 0-85059-548-7

The manufacturers, suppliers and distributors
mentioned in this book are the personal choices of the
contributors. There are other manufacturers and
products on the market. The reader should note that,
as this book went to press, the future of Airfix was
still uncertain. Whilst the contributors hope that
Airfix products will continue to be available, it is not
possible to be sure of this.

Text photoset in 9 on 10 pt English Times
by Manuset Limited, Baldock, Herts.
Printed in Great Britain on 90 gsm Fineblade coated
cartridge, and bound, by The Garden City Press,
Letchworth, Herts, for the publishers,
Patrick Stephens Limited, Bar Hill, Cambridge,
CB3 8EL, England.

one only £2.50

Introduction

I was naturally very pleased to be invited to edit this new book from PSL and, after accepting, I gave a good deal of thought to the choice of contents. My aim was to select articles which would be of as much interest and practical use as possible for the majority of readers, while covering the major aspects of the hobby in a balanced presentation. All railway modellers particularly like to read about layouts built by other enthusiasts, of this there can be no doubt! Certainly such features are not only interesting and entertaining but can also provide much in the way of ideas and information for the readers' own modelling activities. I am therefore delighted to be able to include descriptions, photographs and track plans of four layouts, all excellent, each with its own features of special interest, and providing a good variety. Mike Walshaw has complemented the description of his Westport Branch layout with a further contribution, explaining the details of operation. The system he has devised can be applied with suitable modifications to any layout and will provide continuing entertainment from a model railway after construction is complete.

We are very fortunate today in the high quality and wide variety of ready-to-run and kit locomotives and rolling stock available and most modellers utilise these products rather than building such items from scratch. With this in mind, the articles on locomotives and rolling stock emphasise the choice, detailing and conversion of these models. In addition to general advice and information there are two step by step construction features, for the unusual Class 13 shunting locomotive and for a BR stone wagon. For most enthusiasts it is with the structures and scenery that there is the greatest scope for creativity and individuality. Structure modelling also forms an excellent introduction to scratch-building techniques. I have, therefore, deliberately devoted quite a large section of the book to these aspects of railway modelling. Again there is a mixture of general advice, including an article by master structure modeller, Allan Downes, and specific projects that you can model yourself.

I would like to thank all those modellers who have contributed articles to this book and those who have allowed me to use pictures of their models to illustrate various points. Compiling this book has given me a great deal of pleasure and I have made several new friends as a result; I hope that you will gain as much enjoyment from reading it!

Michael Andress

Contents

Westport Station, SR

M.H. Walshaw

History

Westport Station has a longer history than most model railways; it dates back to 1951, just three years after the 'Big Four' companies had been nationalised. At that time I was 15, and a move of home had forced me to scrap my first 00-gauge layout—an incomplete immovable affair, laid on warped kitchen tables. As I could see that further moves would occur over the years I decided that a 'transportable' layout, which did not fit the walls of a particular room, should avoid further acts of destruction. The fact that the basic layout design, and even some of the original 1951 baseboards, have survived five moves of room or home testifies to the success of this decision. Over this period, of course, virtually everything else has been renewed—the track and wiring, the locos and rolling stock, the scenery and most of the buildings—as my modelling standards and the quality of

proprietary models and kits improved. The imagined location of Westport has moved too, from Lancashire to the Dorset coast between Swanage and Weymouth.

Having set the scene, then, I will describe the main aspects of the layout, concentrating on those where Westport claims to be a little bit different from the ordinary.

Layout concept and design

Having become bored with 'tail-chasing' on my first layout, and inspired by contemporary modellers like P.R. Wickham and F.G. Roomes, I adopted the basic concept of the terminal station and hidden storage sidings. Whilst this concept was relatively novel in 1951 it has subsequently become very popular for both private and club layouts. My aim of fitting into any room (within limits!) obliged me to adopt a deep solid 'island' baseboard format,

Fig 1 *The track plan of Westport station and the hidden storage sidings. The thicker dashed lines are covered tracks and the thinner ones baseboard breaks. The position of all the signals is shown, although at the time of writing only the extreme left-hand signal is installed.*

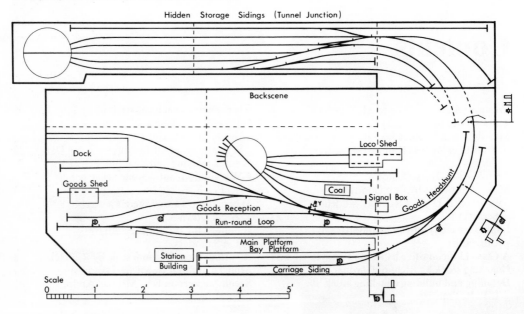

Hidden   Storage   Sidings   (Tunnel Junction)

Backscene

Dock

Goods Shed

Loco Shed

Coal

Signal Box

Goods Reception

Run-round Loop

Goods Headshunt

Main Platform
Bay Platform

Station
Building

Carriage Siding

Scale
0   1'   2'   3'   4'   5'

rather than a long thin I, L, U or hollow square. For access reasons the solid island must not be too large, and I chose an overall size of 5 ft × 9 ft 6 in.

As will be seen from the plan (Fig 1), the station occupies the front three feet, the town section the next foot and the hidden sidings the rear foot of depth (1, 2 and 3). The main line curve was set at 2 ft-radius (somewhat sharp for modern scale models) and the pointwork was designed to maximise and equalise the lengths of the main platform line, the goods reception and the principal storage lines to accommodate trains of up to four coaches or 12 goods vehicles. The station was also given a bay platform line, a carriage siding, a common run-round line (a bit of a luxury, perhaps, but very useful when a dense exhibition service is being run), a generous loco yard (4) and a three-road goods yard. With a few minor additions the station is precisely as it was designed in 1951 but the hidden sidings have been considerably extended from their original three.

The layout was originally designed for one-man (boy) operation, with the control point at the front (5). Whilst the station points were, and still are, manually operated from lever frames, the hidden points and turntable were electrically controlled from a control panel at the front of the layout. 'Track-circuiting' was also introduced to indicate on this panel the track sections which were occupied. However, as I now have a son and other helpers to run the layout at both ends, the control panel for the hidden sidings is normally sited at the rear of the layout (6).

Baseboards

The less said about the baseboards the better, since hardboard on a frame of $1\frac{1}{2}$ in × $\frac{3}{4}$ in timber was originally used. Some still exists, but most has since been replaced. The baseboards are in five sections, of which the clumsiest are 5 ft × 2 ft 3 in and 3 ft 6 in × 3 ft. Each rests on four legs, consisting of two inverted U-frames, braced apart, and everything bolts together with 68 coach bolts. No precision location dowels are used between the baseboards since, with a little slop in the bolt holes, the 27 track joints can easily be aligned before the wing-nuts are tightened right up.

Trackwork

The original track was Graham Farish 'Formo', laid with an outside third conductor rail. After changing to 2-rail in 1961, I gradually replaced this with GEM 'Flexi-Trak' and hand-built

points with copper-clad Paxolin sleepering. The main lines are ballasted with granulated cork, fixed with Shellac knotting, and the sidings with various mixes of N-gauge ballast and powder colours fixed with diluted PVA adhesive. Realistic track painting is a vital finishing touch and several special mixes of Floquil matt paints were devised for the rails and sleepers.

The hidden turntable is based on a Modelcraft design and is actuated automatically to position itself for whichever line the points are set for. The station turntable was originally a simple affair soldered up from rail and a treacle tin, but this was replaced by a scratch-built model based on an L & SWR design. It employs a small geared servomotor under the deck to drive it round on the circular rail laid in the well.

Locos and rolling stock

Being a 'layout person' rather than a 'stock builder', I was initially content to purchase proprietary locos and stock so that a reasonable service could be run as soon as the track was laid. Gradually, as more stock was acquired, extra hidden storage sidings were laid to accommodate it. As little space now remains for further extension, the maximum capacity of the layout has been reached and the stock list comprises eight steam locos, 16 bogie passenger carriages, four non-passenger coaching stock, one diesel rail bus (with a noise-producing 'free motor', described in Reference 1) and 45-50 goods vehicles.

Initially, everything was of Hornby-Dublo manufacture, but other proprietary items appeared later. Kit-built items have also been introduced, starting with Peco's 'Wonderful' wagons and progressing through coaches to locos, the current policy being to replace all the inappropriate or low standard stock with nicely detailed substitutes. The opportunity is also being taken to concentrate on stock appropriate to an ex-L & SWR branch line in late SR days.

One train warrants particular mention. In order to increase the operational interest of the layout an imaginary off-stage branch to connect with extensive Army sidings at Lulworth Camp has been introduced. All the Army traffic has to travel via Westport, where the trains reverse, and the latest loco to be commissioned is therefore a War Department 'Austerity' 0-6-0ST, built from an old Airfix kit and finished in WD dull green livery. It generally hauls a train of low machinery wagons loaded with World War II tanks, with an SR-pattern brake van in WD livery on the tail (7). Automatic couplings and remote uncoupling facilities have long been an

1 *A general view from the station throat. The 'King Arthur' 4-6-0 waits in the bay platform with a through train to Waterloo, while an M7 0-4-4T has just brought in a Pullman 'special' for the Generals' annual visit to Lulworth Camp.*

2 *A general view from the loco headshunt, showing the goods yard. The first ground disc signal to be installed is in the foreground.*

3 *A general view of the hidden storage sidings. The two freight trains in the foreground actually extend under the raised ground shown in photograph 10.*

4 *The loco yard showing the 65 ft L&SWR-pattern turntable, the ancient kit-built water tower and the 'stone' built loco shed and coaling stage. A freight train is being marshalled on the goods reception line.*

5 *Westport console showing the track panel, the signal-box telephone, the sequence cards on the split-rings, the section-switch box and the electronic controller.*

6 *The control console for the hidden sidings, showing the track panel with the track-circuit and route lamps, the pack of sequence cards and a corner of the automatic turntable.*

7 *The WD 'Austerity' 0-6-0ST brings in a train of Army tanks from Lulworth Camp while the M7 0-4-4T and push-pull set wait in the bay platform.*

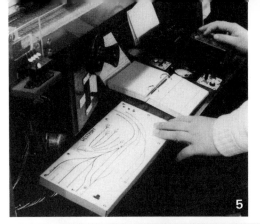

essential feature at Westport, with its constant need for running-round, shunting and remarshalling. Since I started off with Hornby-Dublo stock I have adopted exclusively the Peco pattern of coupling as fitted to post-war Hornby-Dublo stock. Given careful mounting, shaping and polishing, with the aid of home-made jigs and gauges (described in Reference 2), the coupling has proved to be very reliable in service. The latest development is to use Kadee uncoupling magnets, glued down between the rails, to provide uncoupling facilities in certain sidings in lieu of the mechanically controlled uncouplers described in the Reference.

Signalling

As a railway signal enthusiast as well as a modeller, I regret that so few model railways incorporate correctly placed and functioning model signals. The reason is simply that, unless the signals are really built into the track-switching system, they are a mere frill as far as running the layout is concerned, where one and the same person sets the route and drives the trains. A glance at the photographs accompanying this article will, I am afraid, confirm the point, since until recently trackwork, electrics

and scenery have taken precedence over the signals.

Signalling is the next in priority, however, and, with advice from the Signalling Record Society, the proper signal layout has been schemed out (Fig 1). It is intended to model L & SWR lower-quadrant semaphores for the running signals and Westinghouse SR ground discs for the shunt signals. It will be seen that the only Down semaphores are the home signals, on a three-doll bracket, whilst there are two sets of Up signals: the platform starters and the advanced starter/shunt ahead/distant for the next box (named Tunnel Junction). Besides these, eight ground discs will be required to control those shunting movements which affect the running lines.

The signals will be actuated by sub-miniature relays and will be interlocked with the relevant points and with each other so that conflicting routes cannot be signalled. They will be controlled to the 'clear' position by push-buttons arranged 'geographically' on the control panel but will automatically return to 'danger' when the train has moved past. Thus the work-load on the driver/signalman will be reduced as far as possible.

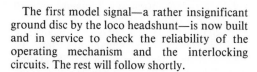

8   *Westport station building with the diesel railbus 'ticking over' while the G6 0-6-0T shunts the yard.*

9   *Westport Bay with the Isle of Portland in the distance. A small coaster unloads timber in Westport Dock, served by a private siding.*

10   *The hilly end of Westport, where the main line has to tunnel under the town. The sloping ground behind the trees is to be turned into allotments one day.*

The first model signal—a rather insignificant ground disc by the loco headshunt—is now built and in service to check the reliability of the operating mechanism and the interlocking circuits. The rest will follow shortly.

Buildings and scenery

For many years only the essential railway buildings had been modelled and a crude back-scene hid the storage sidings. The station building was of freelance design modelled in card (8), the goods shed was made from a Bilteezi kit (2), the loco shed from Ossett mouldings (4) and the L & SWR-pattern signal-box from a Prototype kit (1).

Then the time came to make a dioramic representation of the town of Westport and its back-drop of Dorset coastal hills. Seeking a quicker solution than scratch-building (so that I could get on with the signals), I chose the Super-quick range for the modelled buildings and Hamblings' back-scene sheets for the more distant ones. The back-drop hills were painted on a separate plane of thick card. The whole was then 'framed' by a sky-painted backscene rising 18 in above the foreground level so as to remove from view the usual behind-the-scenes clutter of faces, controllers, coffee cups, etc (4, 9 and 10).

Electrics

I mentioned earlier that the layout is now normally operated by two people, one at the front in charge of Westport and the other at the rear in charge of Tunnel Junction. Each operator normally controls only his local tracks, but trains traversing the main line from one to the other are driven all the way on the receiving controller. To do this, the receiving operator presses a key-switch which gives him control of the departure tracks. To facilitate this co-operative working between the two operators and to obviate the need for shouting, prototype SR block signalling instruments and bells are used, so the operators really do have to be signalmen, 'offering' and 'accepting' trains on the main line and using the proper SR bell codes.

11 *The SR train describer, with illuminated lamps indicating 'Fast Passenger' 'DOWN-From' and 'Waterloo'.*

The track-circuiting of the hidden storage sidings, originally installed for one-boy operation, utilises a circuit once marketed by the NMRA (USA). It is a DC relay circuit, with miniature resistors across the wheels of vehicles to be detected. It will detect the presence of single vehicles or locos, moving or isolated, and has proved very reliable. The detection relays for the 20 track-circuit sections illuminate red lamps on the panel to indicate when they are occupied (6).

Finally, to simplify the task of the Tunnel Junction driver/signalman, his 13 pairs of points are controlled not by individual switches but by 'entrance-exit' route-setting push-buttons on the panel (6). Thus by simply pressing a pair of buttons he can set up a complete route through the pointwork. Contacts on the relays which are used to actuate the points also direct the automatic turntable, switch the frog polarity, isolate all routes not set and illuminate white route lamps on the panel.

Operation, exhibiting and presentation

Gradually, as appropriate stock has been accumulated, a sequence of movements has been devised to represent a prototypical day's operation. Thus the branch push-pull train shuttles between Westport and the main line, through trains run to and from Waterloo and through coaches off Waterloo-Weymouth trains run in on the tail of the push-pull. Army troop and tank trains transit through and Westport's daily freight visits to shunt the yard. A separate article describing how the model train service was devised, and giving details of the sequence

cards to be seen in photographs 5 and 6, will be found in the next section.

Having largely completed the layout, I have started venturing out with it to the occasional model railway exhibition in the district. The presence of an operator at the front is most unusual in exhibition layouts, but it does afford the onlooker a rare chance to see the controls in action. The backscene completely hides the Tunnel Junction operator from view and necessitates a telephone for the occasional oral communication when things go astray (5).

Since the trains are not run aimlessly, it was felt that the onlooker might be interested in knowing what is supposed to be happening. A map of the local railway geography is therefore displayed, together with an SR train describer, appropriately captioned, with its indicator lamps worked from a switch-box behind the scenes (11).

Finally, on the important matter of presentation, the station area is properly lit by floodlamps cantilevered out over it, since the lighting in so many halls leaves much to be desired. Also, great efforts have been made to tidy up the baseboard edge with dark brown paint and protective Perspex strips, beneath which curtains hide the multitude of legs and wires.

Conclusion

The continued development of Westport has given me and my helpers much pleasure over the years; indeed it has proved to have much more development potential for its size than I ever imagined. Exhibition attendance always spurs on the latest improvement and encourages careful attention to reliability, fault eradication and competent operation.

Finally, I must thank my long-suffering wife for her understanding of the demands of my hobby and acknowledge Michael Andress for the fine photographs which illustrate this article. ●

References

1 'More on Free Motors, or Does Your Diesel Tick Over?', *Model Railway News*, Vol 45, March 1969, p 126.

2 'Improved Uncouplers and Peco-style Coupling', *Model Railway Constructor*, Vol 40, January 1973, p 24.

Train service modelling

M.H. Walshaw

It hardly needs saying that railways were built for the purpose of carrying traffic and that a train service has therefore to be devised for each line to enable it to do this. The types of service vary tremendously, from the basic 'as and when required' trips on a quarry railway with two locos and a dozen tip trucks, to the highly complex pattern of express, semi-fast and stopping services that radiate out of Waterloo Station on the Southern Region of BR. The modelling of a realistic train service for one's model railway layout is therefore a valid and worthwhile branch of the hobby, and one that can add a great deal of interest for the operator and spectator alike. It can also involve a degree of historical research and demand the provision of particular items of motive power and rolling stock.

The main objective in train service modelling is to devise a realistic pattern of train moves, either as a sequence or as a timetable, expressed in the form of written instructions for the operators. The aim of this article is to show just what can be done on the common layout design consisting of a terminal station and a set of hidden storage sidings. Westport Station, the subject of the preceding article in this book, is taken as the main illustration of the ideas which are to be described.

Preliminaries—layout concept and the 'scenario'

In the first stages of layout design one has to decide upon what 'piece of railway' one is modelling. For example, it may be main line or branch line; open track or junction; through, junction or terminal station, etc. Largely this is a question of available space and modelling scale, but it does greatly influence the type and complexity of train service that can be operated.

Then one comes to the detailed design of the track layout, in which the needs of the train service should be considered in terms of traffic-handling facilities such as passenger platforms, loading docks, goods sheds, coal drops, etc, and ancillaries like carriage sidings, running loops and loco coaling, watering and stabling facilities.

In terms of modelling the train service, two *basic layout concepts* can be considered: *a)* The fully modelled, multi-station, 'complete' railway, where trains do not disappear behind the scenes to imagined destinations and *b)* The one- or two-station layout where trains do depart to imagined destinations. My Westport layout, with more hidden than visible train accommodation, typifies this layout concept. An interesting variant is to have two connected terminal stations, 'A' and 'B', with a scenic break between them, representing stations many miles away from each other on the company's network. Thus a train leaving station 'A' destined for 'X' (off-scene) arrives at station 'B' as having originated from 'Y' (off-scene).

The ideas to be described can be applied to either of these basic layout concepts, although *(b)* perhaps offers more scope for strict realism.

The next aspect to look at is the 'scenario', by which I mean the complete setting for the railway. The main points which need to be settled before the train service can be modelled are the following:

1 The period represented and the company or companies operating the line, eg:

The 1870s — many independent concerns.

The 1930s — the 'Big Four' with scope for a wide variety of services from the 'pick-up' goods to the luxury express.

The 1950s — the BR pre-Beeching steam and diesel era, with many interesting contrasts.

The 1980s — the 'modern image' BR electric and diesel era, with simplified track layouts, rationalised services and colourful freight trains.

2 The geographical location of the line, industrial/inland country/coastal and city/town/village.

3 The piece of railway that has been modelled (as determined by the layout design), together with what, in layout concept (*b*), lies behind it in the imagination.

To illustrate the foregoing, here is the scenario of my own Westport Station. The station serves

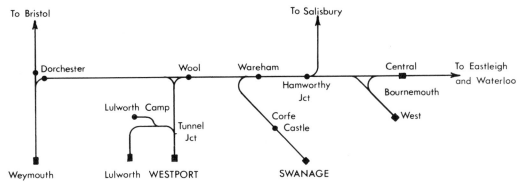

Fig 1 *Block plan of South-East Dorset, showing the imaginary Westport Branch and the former Swanage Branch.*

an imaginary town on the Dorset coast between Swanage and Weymouth. The period is the early to mid-1950s. The piece of railway modelled is simply Westport Station, but the imagined system to which the Westport Branch is connected is somewhat more extensive, as is shown by the 'block plan' in Fig 1.

Devising the train service

With the scenario defined, the stage is now set for us to devise a realistic train service to carry the traffic on offer. We start by providing a pattern of long distance and cross country services at appropriate times of the day and then fit in the local trains, with morning and evening peak services for the commuters. Newspapers, parcels and perishable traffics have their own

patterns of service, often operating at night or in the early morning. Freight services are then fitted in when there is space for them; and one should not forget that they come in many varieties, such as: general merchandise in through, pick-up or short trip workings; mineral trains, full or empty; through block trains, eg oil tankers or containers; and special trains for, say, the Army, a circus on the move, or for the Permanent Way Department. Finally come the uneconomic movements of empty stock and light engines, common enough on the prototype but often forgotten on the model. They should all, however, have some purpose.

This is where the research comes in, for we are trying to model what does, did, or might have happened. The 'modern image' man has merely

Fig 2 *Train service graph for the Swanage Branch for summer weekdays in 1956 for the period from 5.00 am to 2.00 pm. (The block plan of the area is shown in Fig 1.) The branch was single-track from its junction with the main line, a mile beyond Wareham to Swanage, apart from a passing loop at Corfe Castle, therefore trains cannot cross each other on the branch except at Corfe Castle. Many of the branch trains provide connections with Weymouth-Bournemouth trains, but for clarity the latter are not shown. The variety of trains and the random nature of their timings is an obvious feature of the service; indeed at times trains follow each other Down the branch at quarter-hour intervals.*

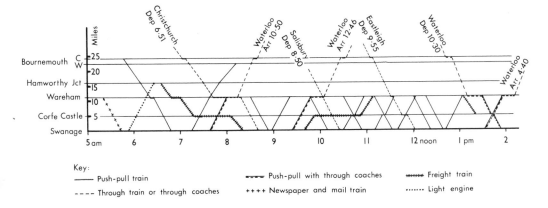

to spend 24 hours by the lineside observing what goes on (and understanding why!), but the historical man must search for old Working Timetables or traffic descriptions in the magazines to determine the operating pattern typical of the line being modelled. For example, the train service at Westport is based loosely on what used to happen at Swanage, a few miles to the East.

Fig 2 shows, in the form of a train graph, part of the Summer Weekday service on the Swanage branch line in 1956. Over the day, there were 16 return workings by the two branch push-pull trains. Of these, the 7.15 am Up departure and the 6.00 pm Down arrival were extended through from Wareham, the junction station, to and from Bournemouth to provide the 'commuter' services. Some of the push-pull trains also conveyed through coaches for Swanage detached from Waterloo to Weymouth trains at Wareham. These through coaches had to be stabled overnight at Swanage before returning to Waterloo because the Down through coaches arrived at 1.54, 7.52 and 9.42 pm after the departure of the Up through coaches at 7.38, 9.24 am and 1.33 pm.

A newspaper and mail train was the first arrival of the day, whilst later in the morning the daily freight train made its leisurely way down the branch and back to Wareham. There were also through trains from Salisbury and Eastleigh. On summer Saturdays one of the through coach/push-pull workings in each direction was replaced by two complete through trains between Waterloo and Swanage and, late on Friday evenings, a train of empty coaches arrived from Bournemouth to provide the required stock. Light engine movements were created by the early morning newspaper and mail train, by the Friday evening empty stock train, by the return Salisbury train and by one of the Saturday trains from Waterloo. Otherwise light engine movements on the branch were avoided by double-heading the push-pull trains.

The traffic pattern on the Swanage line was probably more complex and interesting than one might have imagined for a ten-mile single-track branch. It is hoped therefore that this description will have given the modeller some idea of how to devise his own train service, or to utilise the prototype's, and how to plot this on a train graph.

Track allocation

Most modellers tend to acquire more locos and rolling stock than they really have room for. After devising the basic train service, the modeller is then faced with the very real problem of working out exactly where to run or store each of his trains. As an illustration from Westport, an excursion train arrives with day-trippers from Bristol. There is nowhere in Westport to store the empty stock during the day because at times the two platform lines are occupied by the push-pull train and a Waterloo through train, whilst the carriage siding is occupied by the stock of the early morning newspaper and mail train. (See photograph 1 of the accompanying article on Westport Station). The empty excursion train has therefore to be removed to imagined sidings at Tunnel Junction to keep the station clear.

In a very simple service one can work out the track allocations just by running the trains, but

Move No.	Tunnel Jct		1		2	3	4		
	Westport		1	2	3	4	5		
Tunnel Junction	Turntable			KA					
	Siding 1			SR3			KA & SR3		
	Siding 2	AT & Frt							
	Siding 3	PP & M7							
Westport Station	Main platform	SR3 & KA							
	Bay platform	Pcls & G6				PP & M7			
	Carriage siding			Pcls & G6					
	Goods reception				Frt		Frt & AT		
	Run-round loop				AT				

Fig 3 *Track occupancy chart. Each track is given its own row, in which a vertical line denotes a change of occupancy. The sequence of moves progresses from left to right. In this simplified example, based on the layout shown in Fig 1 of the article on Westport station, the service commences with the 'Austerity Tank' (AT) on a freight train occupying hidden siding 2 at Tunnel Junction and the push-pull (PP) with the M7 0-4-4T at its rear occupying siding 3. In Westport station the 'King Arthur' (KA) stands at the head of an SR 3-coach set (SR3) in the main platform while the G6 0-6-0T waits in the bay platform with the parcels train.*

In the first joint move, the 'King Arthur' travels over the main line to Tunnel Junction's siding 1, where the loco uncouples and moves onto the turntable. It must wait here for a clear road before it can run round its train. In Westport's Move 2, the G6 shunts the parcels train to the carriage siding. When it has done so, Tunnel Junction sends the 'Austerity Tank' and its freight train to Westport where they run into the goods reception line, the loco then uncoupling and proceeding to the run-round loop to wait for the next move to be completed. This is when the M7 propels its push-pull train from Tunnel Junction's siding 3 to the bay platform.

After this the two operators can act independently for a while, Tunnel Junction running the King Arthur round the SR 3-set and Westport running the 'Austerity Tank' round on to the tail of its freight in the goods reception. And so it goes on.

in a more complex case it is better to do this on paper first. Fig 3 shows how this was done on the Westport Branch, using a modified train graph to show the occupancy of each track. An alternative is to move slips of paper, scaled to the lengths of the trains, around on a scale track plan. This method will help to ensure that long trains are not allocated to short tracks. This was a very important aspect of track allocation on the Westport Branch since the hidden storage sidings are often completely filled with less than an inch to spare.

Another consideration in preparing the train schedule is to ensure that every loco and set of carriages gets back to its original starting point at the end of the day's operations. The same does not go for goods wagon movements, however, and these may be randomly selected each day by cutting a pack of playing cards, throwing dice or even by means of a computer! Freight traffic modelling is really beyond the scope of this article though.

Operators' instruction cards

The operators of the layout need to have written instructions telling them what trains to run, where and when. A simple list-type format was tried at Westport, but under exhibition conditions it was found that the operators tended to lose their places rather too easily. A sequence card format was therefore designed, one card being used for each batch of moves by each loco in turn. The card details the stock that the loco is to draw, as well as giving light-engine moves such as running round and shunting. Departure and arrival tracks are specified, together with the necessary section switches or points that must be operated at the beginning of the move to energise the loco and, at the end of the move, to isolate it. A supply of blank cards was first printed with the standard boxes and captions and they were then filled in for each move from the track occupancy chart of Fig 3.

When there are two or more relatively independent operators they must get in phase at

Loco	Move 2 (Wpt 3)			
Austerity Tank	Offer when G6 has shunted parcels train into carriage siding.			
Train	Dep. remarks	From	To	Arr. remarks
Army Frt.		Siding 2	Wpt.	
Bell code	Representing		Dep.	Arr.
2-3	Spl. from Lulworth Camp			

4a

Loco	Move 3 (T.J. 2)			
Austerity Tank				
Train	Dep. remarks	From	To	Arr. remarks
Army Frt.	1, 16, 17, 20	T.J.	Gds. Recep.	U/c loco
L.E.		Gds. Recep.	Loop	1
Bell code	Representing		Dep.	Arr.
2-3	Spl. from Lulworth Camp			1·33pm

4b

2

Figs 4a and b *A pair of typical sequence cards for the Westport Branch relating to the running of the freight train in the sample service of Fig 3 and seen in photograph 7 of the article on Westport station. Fig 4a is Tunnel Junction's card for his Move 2. The cue tells him when to offer the train to Westport (Wpt), which he does with bell code 2-3 ('Is line clear for branch freight train?'). Fig 4b is Westport's corresponding card for his Move 3. When the train has arrived in the goods reception the loco is uncoupled and proceeds light to the loop. In order to set up the route initially, points 1, 16, 17 and 20 had to be changed and, in order to isolate the loco at the conclusion of its move, point 1 had to be changed again.*

2 *The WD 'Austerity' 0-6-0ST heads a train of Army tanks from the fiddle yard. Note the 'driving mirror' in the upper right-hand corner of the photograph. This enables the fiddle yard operator to see what is happening at Westport station.*

times when they have to interact with each other. One can, of course, follow the prototype and run the service to time, but this has obvious disadvantages for exhibition running. On the Westport Branch the aim is to keep the station operator busy and continuously supplied with trains. The operator of the hidden storage sidings exists only to take away Westport's Up trains on demand and to offer Down trains at the right time, ie, just as Westport is completing the previous move. Thus the hidden siding operator needs a 'cue' instruction, telling him at what point in Westport's operations to offer each Down train. Since the hidden siding operator cannot actually see what is happening in the Station because of the backscene, he is given a 'driving mirror' with which to look round the corner. In Figs 4 (a) and (b) are reproduced a pair of sequence cards which relate to the train being run in photograph 7 of the article on Westport Station. These two cards

illustrate the features which have been mentioned, including the cue.

This concludes my description of train service modelling and how it has been applied to the Westport Branch. The present train service, briefly outlined in the Westport article, needs 95 sequence cards for Westport Station and 78 for Tunnel Junction and it takes about three hours to run through a complete day's working. The freight stock circulates to a pre-determined pattern over a three-day cycle. As more representative locos and stock are acquired, the service will be improved to incorporate more prototypical features.

Finally, collective acknowledgment is made to the many modellers whose ideas have contributed to the methods of train service modelling used on the Westport Branch and to Michael Andress for the photograph of a Waterloo through train pulling out of Westport.

●

Mendip Basin N-gauge layout

Romsey & District Railway Modellers Society

Mendip Basin was the first layout of the Romsey & District Railway Modellers Society to be designed and built completely from scratch. Construction started in July 1977 and the layout was first exhibited in September 1979. So far, we have spent about £120 on this layout.

Planning
A considerable amount of discussion took place before the final layout plan was agreed. A main line and a single track layout plan were compared to reach the Mendip Basin compromise.

Layout design
The main features of the design are:
* Double track main line—secondary or cross-country.
* Continuous main line—for maximum action.
* Scale length trains—nine or ten coach trains.
* Spacious layout—large radius points on main line and uncrowded sidings.
* Fairly large radius curves—15-in radius minimum on main line.
* Simple loco facilities—no shed, but water and coal stage, for display of locos.
* Six road traverser—54 in long.
* Modified cab control electrical system—for three controllers.
* Point motors—all points.

In order to meet these requirements, we finished up with a 9 ft × 3 ft layout. The two baseboards were 5 ft × 3 ft & 4 ft × 3 ft, instead of two 4 ft 6 in × 3 ft boards, so that the crossover and long point ladder could be on one board. At the time of construction transport and storage were assured, so the layout was not designed for ease of transport and for prevention of damage on storage.

Scenic design
We tried to take full advantage of the scenic capabilities of N scale. The scenic design can be broken down into several zones:
* Front centre —railway facilities, small station, loco siding, signal box, etc.
* Front left —curved railway bridge over staircase of locks on canal.
* Front right —railway in steep sided cutting, with road overbridge.
* Mid scene —canal as scenic break with (left) staircase of locks; (centre) basin, wharves and sidings and (right) stable and canal tunnel. Like the railway, the canal was to have its associated buildings, lock-keeper's cottage, inn, cottages, timber yard, stone transhipment wharf, stables, etc.
* Back scene —Hills, cliffs and old quarry to give near vertical face behind canal, up to 150 ft high. Village on top of hills planned but not built. Tracks go through tunnels at each end. Sky back scene.

The observer's view was intended to change from one end of the layout to the other to dispel the effect of the train set oval. The overall aim was to show the trains in the landscape, ie to give the impression of looking down on the railway in a valley, with the observer on the other side of the valley. The spacious track layout helps this impression so that the railway appears to belong. Scenic design was helped by drawing an isometric sketch of the layout to give a three dimensional view before construction started. Framing of 4 in deep was necessary instead of the usual 2 in × 1 in framing to get enough depth for the staircase of locks. The hills accounted for about 11 in above the baseboard to give a total baseboard depth of about 16 in.

Location
Mendip Basin is an imaginary location in Somerset. The railway company is joint LM & SR and SR—perhaps a double track link from the S & DR direct to Bristol. Local traffic is stone to the wharf, timber from the timber yard, oil and coal to the fuel depot, fruit to and from

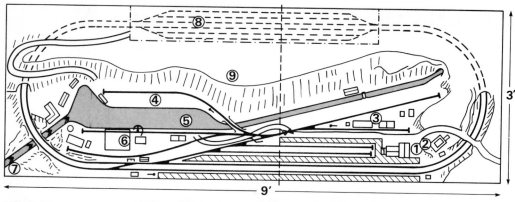

1 Station	4 Stone wharf	7 Staircase of locks
2 Folly	5 Canal basin	8 Storage yard & controls
3 Loco coal & water	6 Timber yard	9 Hills and cliffs (Scale 150' high)

Fig 1 *Mendip Basin.*

the fruit warehouse, and mail from the parcels bay. Some local trains terminate at Mendip Basin too, particularly in the tourist season. It was originally intended to model the village, but it was felt that it would be more typical if the village was sited a mile or so away, off scene. So far no one has identified the precise location of Mendip Basin!

Construction
Baseboards
4 in × 1 in timbers were used. The framing consisted of three longitudinal members at 1 ft 6 in apart with cross members 1 ft apart. High quality smooth surfaced $\frac{1}{2}$ in chipboard was used as cladding. This gave a very strong

and rigid structure. The baseboards are joined with coach bolts and are located with wooden dowels. The canal area was drawn in on the chipboard and cut out with a jig saw; the cut outs were then replaced at a lower level to serve as the canal bed. The area around the staircase of locks was cut out, and the end cross member was cut away so that the cutting around the locks could be modelled. An extra piece of chipboard was inserted at this low level to serve as a base for the lock complex. The two baseboards are quite heavy.

Trackwork
Peco N-Gauge track and points were used with Peco point motors. The track and baseboard

1 *A double-headed freight train crosses the curved viaduct above the staircase of locks with The Navigators pub in the background.*

2 *A small tank engine collects two vans from the fruit warehouse as a coal train passes on the main line.*

were drilled with a small drill in a pin chuck, and track was pinned down with brass track-pins. At the baseboard joint, the rails were soldered on to brass screws, after the heights had been adjusted. Tracksetta templates were used to ensure accurate track-laying and good running on the 15 in radius curves. The rails were painted before ballasting. Granite ballast was sprinkled in place, then PVA, diluted with water containing detergent and black powder paint, was applied with a medicine dropper.

Storage yard (I) Traverser
A 54 in long, 9 in wide piece of chipboard was used as the base. Side members of 2 in × 1 in wood were screwed on to give rigidity. Oak blocks were screwed to the underside of the board to slide on fixed metal rails. Six parallel tracks were laid, four of them halved electrically so that they could take two trains. Copper-clad plastic strips were screwed to the ends of the traverser and the traverser tracks were soldered to the copper-clad plastic.

Storage yard (II) Fiddle yard
Because the traverser restricted operation, it was decided to change the traverser board to a plug-in fiddle yard, complete with points. The six tracks were relaid as up and down main lines with two storage loops each way to give six tracks. The board is screwed into place for running, and electrical connections are via a multi-pin plug and socket.

Controls
The central control panel carries section and controller selection switches. The points are operated via stud and electric pencil panels—there are duplicate panels at each end of the layout. This is to avoid operator congestion behind the layout. Connections between the two baseboards are via a flat multi-way connector.

Scenery
The basis is expanded polystyrene, held in place with ceiling tile adhesive. The expanded polystyrene was then carved into shape (with the bread knife!); smoothly for the hills and banks and roughly for the rocks. A mixture of filler, PVA adhesive, powder colours and water was daubed with a brush. While the scenic goo was still wet, scatter materials were sprinkled on. Paths were made by going over the surface with a wet paint brush before the mixture had set. Since the scenic goo was made up in small batches, and the mix and amount of colours varied, a realistic variation in tone and tint was seen in the earth and rocks. The rocks were further treated by pouring on dilute solutions of powder colours and letting the liquid flow down. The quarry face was applied quite thickly and smoothed before carving in the lines of strata. When dry the quarry face was treated the same as the rocks. Scatter material was blown on so that it lodged in the crevices. This technique gives instant scenery—it is quite fascinating to see the transformation from white expanded polystyrene into finely detailed hills and rocks. It takes about half an hour to an hour for the scenic base to set hard.

Canal
Clear polyester encapsulating resin was used to represent the water. The canal bed was painted dark green/brown before the first cast was made. After the first cast had set, the surface was roughly brushed with dark oak wood stain to give a murky appearance, then the final cast was made. A few grass seed heads were embedded to give the effect of reeds. Just before the resin had set, the barges were embedded and scatter material was dusted around the banks. The final effect is realistic—in places the water looks quite deep. A few weeks after casting, a coat of gloss varnish was brushed on to give the stagnant canal water effect.

Structures
The canal lock assembly was made from display card, carefully measured to fit the site. The paving stones were made by scribing on manilla card folder material which was then 'washed' with dirty thinners. Lock gates, beams and steps were all built from balsa sheet. Space was left for the tow path, surfaced with Faller HO embossed card cobble-stones. The effect of water leaking through the closed lock gates was produced with gloss varnish highlighted with white paint.

The viaduct over the locks was again built from display card, covered with N brick paper. The bridge girder section in the centre was fabricated from Peco N concrete platform edging and the handrails came from an American N diesel loco. The road overbridge was cut out to fit the site. It also is display card covered with N brickpaper. A similar sloping overbridge may be seen near Winchester station. After these structures had been put in place the sites were filled in with expanded polystyrene coated with scenic goo and scatter material as before.

3 Another view of the canal basin, showing also the quarry face at the rear. The Q1 locomotive heading the train in the foreground was built by Richard Wiltshire.

4 The stone trans-shipment wharf and quarry face.

5 Richard Wiltshire's model of a Peckett industrial locomotive hauls three wagons from the private siding. Note the gates.

6 Mendip Basin signal box is a scratch-built model. The Southern S15 locomotive is another of Richard Wiltshire's models.

7 The 'Western Oils' fuel depot.

8 The station area with two LMS 2-6-2T locomotives in charge of passenger trains. The engine coal and water facilities are behind the station with the canal at the rear and the stable on the tow path.

7

8

Buildings

The station building is based on *Railway Modeller* drawings of Totton (L & SWR) station. A manilla folder card was laminated in three layers, so that depth for doors and windows could be obtained, and covered with N brick paper. UHU adhesive was used since (aqueous) PVA was found to weaken and discolour the brick paper and took longer to dry. The roof was covered with N slate paper. Chimney top details were made from stripped wire insulation, stuck in Blu-tac, then painted. The awning was planked (1 mm) Plastikard, with the station name applied with Blik Dryprint. The waiting shelter was a quickie in laminated Plastikard, based on drawings of Wool (L & SWR) in *Model Railway Constructor*. The platform flagged surface is 00 brick embossed plastic sheet, covered with a thin coating of grey scenic goo. The water tank structure is based on *Model Railway Constructor* drawings of that at Wimborne Minster (L & SWR). Laminated construction, like the station, was used. The tank was made from Plastikard and filled with varnish. Creepers were modelled by applying streaks of UHU to the sides of the building and then blowing on scatter material. The coaling stage was built from planked Plastikard and balsa and is based on photographs of the coaling stage at Yeovil (L & SWR). The signal box is a foreigner, the prototype being at Cottingham, near Hull (NER) and the drawings were published in the *Railway Modeller*. This particular box was chosen since instead of continuous glazing there were windows separated by brick panels so that a strong laminated structure could be produced. The roof was covered by slate paper, nicked to give the effect of individual slates—this appeared to be wasted effort in N scale since the roof looks no better than plain slatepaper! The complex glazing was modelled very easily by using Blik Dryprint white lines on Clear Plastiglaze. The finish is very neat and there is enough relief to give the effect of glazing bars, and, no

painting is needed. The same glazing technique was used for the station buildings.

The Navigation Inn and towpath stables were a rapid conversion of the Builder Plus farm. The sides were coated with thick white poster colour. Window and door surrounds were cut from paper, painted and glued in place. Roofing was 00 brick embossed plastic sheet painted a purple tinge to represent West Country slate. The lockkeeper's cottage and the other cottages were also adapted from Builder Plus kits; this time the sides were painted with grey scenic goo. The roofs were the same as the Inn. The fruit warehouse was another Builder Plus product, this time built as instructed. The change on this was scribing the corrugated iron print with an aluminium pencil, followed by careful weathering.

The stone wharf was embellished with a demounted van body, as an office, and conveyors built from scrapbox pieces. The heaps of stone were modelled by sticking lumps of polystyrene foam to the baseboard, then coating with dry stone scatter material. The scatter material was then coated with diluted PVA and detergent, as for ballasting. These buildings were built by our Secretary, Howard Coulson. Our Vice Chairman, Richard Wiltshire, provided an impressive collection of buildings, as follows. Wiltshire Timber, the timberyard, was built from Plastruct Girders roofed with lead foil, from wine bottles. The timber stacks were balsa scrap. The fuel depot complex was built from scrap, the oil tanks are from Lima N tank wagons, and the coal bins are balsa strips. (It is quite common for static storage tanks to be built from demounted road or rail tankers.) The dominating folly was built from thick card and was ivyclad with adhesive and scatter material. When the scenery was built, a knoll had to be incorporated as the base for the folly. The road/rail canal overbridge and the drawbridge over the canal were built from scrap. The numerous small huts and water cranes were built and painted by our junior members.

Detailing

Trees

Some trees were made from garden twigs—dipped in varnish then sprinkled with green scatter material, the operation repeated if necessary. The large masses of trees were made from lichen—the lichen was fixed in place with staples and then sprayed with diluted varnish, followed by dusting with scatter material, repeated if necessary. Bushes were modelled in the same way. Gorse was modelled by taking small ragged pieces of lichen, dipping in varnish and dusting with green scatter material. These green shrubs were fixed in position then dotted with varnish followed by dusting with yellow scatter material. Heather was represented by dusting with purple scatter material, stuck with dilute PVA.

General

Several yards of fencing were used, mostly proprietary, of several types to give variety. Richard Wiltshire also built some soldered jig-built fencing and some post and wire fencing to give more variety. He also spent one week of his holidays just before Mendip Basin's first exhibition adding such detail as gardens for the cottages, road surfaces and markings, hoardings, seats, lamp posts, name boards and passengers for the station, oil and coal spills and trackside telegraph poles. Richard also built the canal barges from balsa and lead foil. The incorporation of such detail and clutter adds to the atmosphere, but takes a considerable amount of time and patience.

The last addition was a sky backscene. At present this is plywood covered with sky paper and is designed to drop into slots in the baseboard. However, more detail could be added; a lot more people and animals are needed, a horse on the towpath for example! There is a glaring omission, Mendip Basin has an attractive signal box, but not one signal is to be seen! We have yet to agree on colour light or semaphore signals.

Operation

At its first exhibition, we quickly found that the traverser storage road system limited operation on a double track layout. By its next exhibition the traverser had been replaced by the plug in fiddle yard which permitted independent Up and Down operation of up to five trains each way. When we started all the stock was provided by our Vice Chairman, Richard Wiltshire, from his Hensting Folly layout. Now several members provide stock, but this in itself gives a problem

9 *Mendip Basin station with the Merchant Navy Class locomotive at the head of an express.*

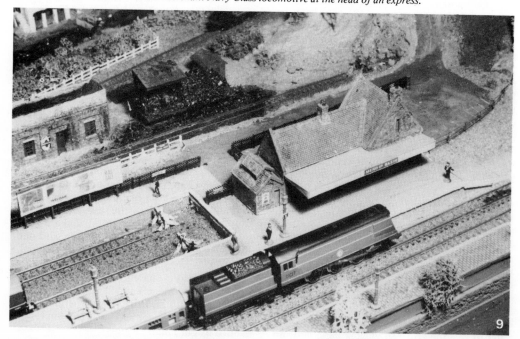

10 *The folly at the rocky end of the layout.*

since we do not know exactly the make up and type of trains. This means sequence or timetable operation is not practised. The aim is to always have one train moving in public view and to always run at scale speeds. We add the odd double-headed train for further interest and try to keep something moving in the wharf sidings. 'Serious' shunting is not attempted because of the difficulty of reliable remote uncoupling with standard N couplings. Whilst the public are well entertained with Mendip Basin, operation is a little tedious and some concentration is needed, but we seem to have no shortage of operators.

To the dismay of some members, but to delight of younger viewers, we include a few diesel hauled trains. The proprietary diesels available can be extremely reliable and can be made to crawl, and will run all day! However, for the steam and SR enthusiasts, Richard Wiltshire does run some of his scratch-built locos such as the Bulleid Q1 in some of the photographs.

We use conventional Hammant & Morgan (non electronic) controllers and do not need to use any electronic track cleaning device. The curves and clearances on the layout are such that they will take just about all available proprietary locos and stock. At club running sessions we have had an American 2-8-8-2 Big Boy Mallet loco round Mendip Basin, German Pacifics and 2-10-0s, all with no problems.

What have we learned from Mendip Basin?
Mendip Basin is difficult to transport and store and is easily damaged in storage but it takes only about 10 to 15 minutes to have it set up and fully operational. The running is very good—any derailments are usually operator error or defective stock—and the scenery is impressive and unusual in British N-gauge layouts.

Mendip Basin was built by beginners
When the Society was started, we had very few experienced modellers, and Richard Wiltshire was our sole experienced N-gauge modeller. Until Richard joined the Society construction was co-ordinated by our Secretary, Howard Coulson, who is an 009 modeller, which perhaps explains the spectacular scenery! After that Richard Wiltshire did the wiring and led the construction team. The scenic techniques were new to everyone, and our Secretary had never made an N-scale building before. Perhaps because we were new to N-scale modelling, we built a rather different layout, from which we all learned a great deal.

On behalf of the Romsey & District Railway Modellers Society, we must thank all those who have helped in any way with the construction, stocking, transport and operation of Mendip Basin. We hope it will inspire both beginners and experienced modellers alike to try something a little out of the ordinary, and also to experiment with scenic and building techniques. ●

Trefolwen

Terry Onslow

Having owned an exhibition layout for four years, I was very aware when I planned my next layout, 'Trefolwen', of what was needed to make an interesting layout. Perhaps the most important thing, first of all, was to choose a place and period on which to base the layout. I wanted to use a wide variety of locomotives and rolling stock, some of which I already owned and some which I wanted to add to my collection. I chose to base my layout on the North Wales/England border in the area around Ruabon, in the 1959-60 period. I felt that this would give me plenty of scope in both stock and operation.

In designing the layout I felt that the usual branch line terminus with a single track approach was operationally limiting so I decided on the idea of featuring both low and high level lines. The low level line depicts an imaginary Cambrian Railways line between Oswestry and Corwen, built during the 1850s. The higher line depicts a Great Western Railway terminus, built in about 1895, from Ruabon. This was constructed primarily to carry stone traffic from the nearby quarries. The GWR had its own station but shared the Cambrian goods yard, linked by a hazardous incline of approximately 1 in 30!

In 1952 the low level line was closed, leaving only a two mile section of track open to serve the quarries. During 1959 the whole area passed from the Western Region to the London Midland Region of British Railways. This allowed the LMR to try out all their new loco-

motives in unusual areas. We now come to the period I have chosen to model—a period when steam and diesel locomotives work together. We see a well used country station with the crumbling ruin of the old Cambrian station on the now little used line below.

I began the layout with baseboards of open top type construction, that is with timber only laid to take the actual trackbed. This allows much more freedom to create realistic contours when the scenery is added later on. All the trackwork is scratch-built as this is not only far more realistic but is also cheaper! It is also very satisfying to build. Track construction utilises SMP parts which comprise copper clad sleepers and rail. When making track a jig is constructed to accept a number of sleepers spaced at the correct intervals. One rail is then soldered on to these sleepers and the unit so formed is pinned or glued into position on the layout. The other rail is then soldered in place. Curves are easily aligned in this way and the gauge is kept correct by the constant use of a track gauge. Pointwork is made on a template and is then laid in position complete. Trackwork on the layout includes a variety of special items—a double slip, two single slips and two 3-way points in the fiddle yard.

I do not enjoy wiring and this aspect, therefore, is kept to a minimum. The whole layout is designed to be one man operated, so all the points, isolating switches, including the fiddle yard, are wired to the main control panel. There are two controllers, one for the main line and

Fig 1 *Trefolwen 4 mm 00-gauge fine scale.*

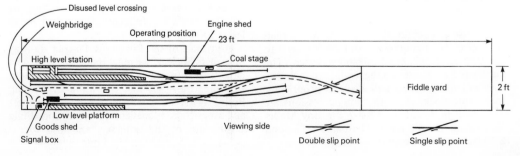

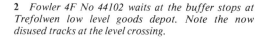

1 *A view of the left-hand end of the layout with the high level station in the background and the low level goods yard in the foreground.*

2 *Fowler 4F No 44102 waits at the buffer stops at Trefolwen low level goods depot. Note the now disused tracks at the level crossing.*

3 *Diesel shunter No 12089 waits as Class 20 D8012 brings in an empty stone train from Flint. Note the disused passenger platform at the low level station.*

4 *GWR 'Prairie' No 5501 pauses at the buffer stops at Trefolwen station. An excursion train is laid off in the siding. The station building is a scratch-built model based on Kemble.*

5 *The ex-LMS 0-6-0 4F No 44102 stands alongside Trefolwen loco shed awaiting the next turn of duty.*

6 *Trefolwen engine shed is on the high level with the low level goods yard in the foreground. The realistic hand-built track includes double and single slip points.*

7 *Class 40 No D279 hauls a train of empty coaching stock into Trefolwen to make up an excursion train.*

one for the lower line and goods yard. The latter can be switched out and the whole layout operated with the main line controller. This facility allows trains to transfer to main line from branch and vice-versa.

With the exception of the Ratio upper quadrant types, all the signals are GWR hand-built models. In the construction of the latter, brass rod is used for the posts and nickel silver for the bases. Colin Waite etched brass arms are utilised with white metal lamps. Brass laddering is purchased in long lengths and is then cut to fit. All the signals are operating and are actuated by Hammant & Morgan point motors or relays; a spring attached to the operating wire of each signal allows them to go back to danger when the point motors are operated. Hammant & Morgan point motors are also used for the points. A microswitch is fitted to each point to eliminate the rather unreliable frog switch on the centre of the motor.

All the buildings are scratch-built. Most are scale models of actual prototypes, adapted to suit the surroundings. The signal-box is based on the one at Highbridge, used for controlling the 90 degree level crossing from the GWR to Somerset & Dorset Railway. The station building is copied from the one at Kemble, Gloucestershire, and the locomotive shed is a shortened version of the shed at Princetown, on Dartmoor. The goods shed is a freelance design of my own. All the buildings were made from Plastikard, backed with balsa wood to prevent warping. I find this material to be the most suitable, having tried various others. Enamel paint was used to colour the buildings whilst white watercolour was employed for the mortar.

The base for the scenery is comprised of wooden blocks screwed to the baseboard cross members and then covered with wire-netting. Mod-Roc is then applied over this, followed by a covering of plaster. This ground surface is painted with earth-brown watercolour and appropriately coloured scatter material is applied. Bushes are modelled from horsehair.

There is a mixture of proprietary and kit-built rolling stock, though the latter is becoming rarer as manufacturers bring out more and more superb ready-to-run models. These usually only need a wheel change and new couplings to become far better than I can build. All stock is well weathered by air-brushing on suitably thinned dirty black paint. On locomotives a touch of white here and there, or a hint of rust dabbed on with a dry brush, makes a tremendous difference to the appearance.

In order to run efficiently it is essential to have a proper timetable. I prepare a sequence rather than a timetable, but the principle is the same. Careful planning is required. The sequence for Trefolwen was devised with the help of many sheets of paper and a suitably numbered track plan, but I managed to arrange for a very comprehensive selection of trains to be run. When I actually ran the layout to the planned sequence only one movement had to be rearranged, so all the preliminary work was worth while! The layout has already been exhibited at several shows and has performed well; the few remaining bugs will be ironed out as time goes by. Building the railway has given me great enjoyment and it is rewarding to see the finished product giving pleasure to others also.

Locomotive roster

K's GWR Pannier Tank 0-6-0 kit. Painted BR black.

Hornby Dublo Class 20. Repainted in BR green and with windscreen wipers fitted.

Jouef Class 40. Repainted and bogie wheels changed for Jacksons.

Class 24. Started life as a Hornby Class 25. Body hacked about and underframe altered. Far more work involved than first imagined! Painted BR green.

Airfix Fowler 0-6-0. Straight off the shelf apart from dirtying-up.

Airfix Prairie. Rewheeled and repainted BR lined green.

Wrenn 0-6-0 Diesel Shunter. Repainted and numbered Class 12 one side and Class 13 the other! The body is moulded this way. As long as you cannot see both sides at once it simply does not matter!

Mainline 'Peak'. Ends modified as a split headcode model. Repainted.

Mainline Collett. Nothing done to it except for dirtying-up.

Mainline Rebuilt Patriot. As above. Used only on excursion trains.

Mainline 'Jubilee'. As above. This locomotive and the Rebuilt Patriot were relined.

Mainline BR 4MT. Relined, but seldom used.

Lima Prairie. New chimney and buffers. Repainted in BR unlined livery.

Hornby 0-6-0 Jinty. Wheels spread to accept finer rail. Repainted in BR unlined black.

Hornby DMU. Fronts rebuilt, new buffers, new underframe, new wheels, and repainted in 1960 livery.

K's GWR 14xx kit. Painted BR unlined black, but rarely used.

Cotswold 16xx Pannier Tank kit. Painted BR unlined black.   ●

Milborne St Giles

Bob Goodwin (Romsey & District Railway Modellers Society)

Setting the scene

Milborne St Giles, a village on the borders of Dorset and Somerset, is the terminus of one of the least known narrow-gauge railways in England. It is a summer Saturday in the late 1930s and the local passenger service has been augmented by a number of special excursion trains bringing day-trippers and ramblers into the local countryside. An occasional stone train from a nearby quarry ambles into the station to reverse before continuing its journey down to the coast. Most of the local trains run 'mixed' with vans and wagons added as required to bring in supplies or to take away the produce of this largely agricultural area. Horses and cars share the narrow country lanes, and a local farmer has just collected one of his pair of steam ploughing engines following minor repairs at the local garage. Near to the station a large mill produces flour and animal feeds; the internal waterwheel quietly drawing power from the passing stream.

Those who seek Milborne St Giles or its railway on the map will look in vain; for one of the attractions of railway modelling in general, and narrow-gauge modelling in particular, is that where a suitable prototype cannot be found, one can simply sit back, indulge in a little fantasy, and invent a railway to model!

Background to the layout

'Milborne' is the fourth narrow-gauge layout which I have built over the past decade or so. Each of its three predecessors followed a simple track plan and included a continuous run as, for a long while, I doubted whether 009/HOe models were reliable enough to give good running in a terminus configuration. The three simple layouts were an invaluable means of developing a wide range of modelling techniques and, once I had mastered the art of making solder-construction points and had produced a reliable uncoupling system, I felt confident that I could finally abandon the continuous run and build a fiddle-yard to terminus layout. One major advantage of the design is that I can extend the layout using additional baseboards as time, and resources, permit.

During this period I had also acquired a variety of rolling stock including locomotives from both the current, and past, manufacturers of narrow-gauge equipment. With very few exceptions I have found good running to be possible with 009/HOe locos, given well-laid track and providing the rails, wheels and pick-ups are all kept scrupulously clean. This statement applies equally to N-gauge mechanisms which are the main source of motive power on 'Milborne', suitably adorned with scratch-built or kit-built bodies.

My previous layouts had all appeared in local model railway shows and I have always enjoyed participating in these events, whether it be in the role of organiser, exhibitor or paying visitor. 'Milborne' was designed from the outset as an exhibition layout and, indeed, apart from test-running, is rarely operated outside of an exhibition hall.

Planning the layout

Careful planning of a model railway layout is the first essential stage in achieving satisfactory end results. This may seem an obvious statement, but one often encounters layouts where the builder seems to have started work with little more than a track plan on the back of an envelope. At the opposite extreme is the modeller who spends all his time planning without ever building anything—but that is another story!

Assuming a choice of scale and gauge has been made, the fundamental questions to be asked are where, how and by whom the layout is to be operated? The answers to these questions should be borne in mind at all stages of the design. To illustrate this point let me offer some examples: an exhibition layout will be designed to be portable with compact, lightweight baseboards, whereas a layout permanently installed in a loft, say, can use larger boards minimising baseboard joints and the consequent electrical connections between boards. A club layout should accommodate a wide selection of stock from various manufacturers and should have a simple control system easily used (and serviced)

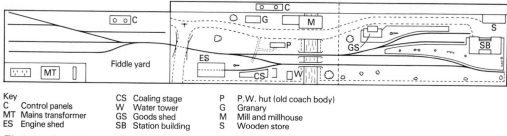

Key

C	Control panels	CS	Coaling stage	P	P.W. hut (old coach body)
MT	Mains transformer	W	Water tower	G	Granary
ES	Engine shed	GS	Goods shed	M	Mill and millhouse
		SB	Station building	S	Wooden store

Fig 1 *A plan of the layout.*

by most club members. In contrast a privately owned layout may be built to more restrictive standards, and perhaps include complex control systems requiring considerable operator experience. As a third example most young modellers find tail-chasing layouts acceptable whilst many adults prefer a more prototypical mode of operation.

As I have already mentioned 'Milborne' is primarily intended for exhibition use, staffed by a small team of experienced operators. The track plan (Fig 1) is, therefore, sufficiently simple to ensure reliable running whilst still allowing a reasonably complex sequence timetable to be run. Thus, hopefully, the layout will both entertain the public and, at the same time, provide sufficient interest and enjoyment for its operators.

The unusually short (3 ft) baseboards were chosen to ensure that the layout will travel comfortably in the back of my small hatchback car and this brought the added advantage that, where necessary, I can carry the two scenic boards, bolted together face to face, single-handed. It will be seen from the plan that provision was made for mounting the mains transformer and the two control panels on the baseboards instead of the alternative approach of using a detachable control unit. Although this reduces the area available for the layout itself this disadvantage is outweighed in an exhibition layout by two important advantages. Firstly, the number of separate items to be carried is reduced and there is less chance of forgetting something when setting out in the early morning. Secondly, the wiring is simplified by reducing the number of possibly unreliable plugs and sockets. As a further refinement the transformer box is designed to store the mains cable whilst in transit and 13 amp extension sockets are mounted in the same box to supply lighting units and a soldering-iron when required.

Throughout the planning phase reliability was, perhaps, the most important consideration. This is reflected in, for example, the choice of

manual point control, the use of new rather than salvaged track from earlier layouts, and the duplication of some of the key electrical circuits. These measures may well cost a few extra pounds but I will consider this money well spent if embarrassing failures in front of the public are avoided.

The final stage in the planning process was to prepare a list of the various stages anticipated in the building of the layout and then to arrange the list in a logical order. Such a list is very valuable in avoiding such pitfalls as ballasting track before platform faces are installed, and also helps to ensure that materials for each stage are purchased in good time!

Basic construction

The baseboards for 'Milborne' were constructed using $\frac{1}{2}$ in thick chipboard mounted on a framework of 2 in × 1 in timber. The boards are linked together and aligned by two $\frac{3}{8}$ in bolts at

Fig 2 *The point control system and wiring.*

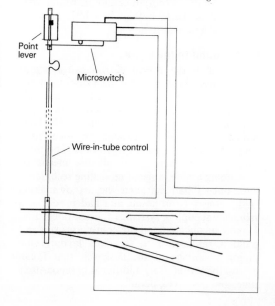

Point lever

Microswitch

Wire-in-tube control

each joint, the timber end-pieces being protected by drilled steel plates. Track was then pinned to the boards using $\frac{1}{16}$ in cork sheet as an underlay, not in this case to reduce noise, but rather to protect the chipboard from excess moisture when ballasting (see below). Trackwork is mainly Peco Crazy Track but 12 in radius hand-made points are used. The points are constructed on SMP 00-gauge copper-clad sleeper strip and, of course, provide the live frogs which are essential for good running with short wheelbase locomotives. Point control is by wire-in-tube from GEM point levers, a micro-switch mounted adjacent to each lever provides switching of polarity at the live frog (Fig 2). Electrical connections to the track feeds were then made using thin multi-strand wire which is inherently less likely to break than the single-strand variety. The control panels were made as small as possible using miniature switches and LED indicator lamps. The two controllers are home-made transistor units employing half-wave rectification for slow-running.

With track laying and wiring complete, an extensive testing programme took place using a wide selection of locomotives and rolling-stock until I was completely satisfied that reliable running would be possible. Once the track has been painted and ballasted, adjustments become very difficult so it is essential to iron out any problems at this stage. If all else fails the track can be relaid completely, but fortunately such drastic measures were unnecessary with 'Milborne'.

The next step was to install the platforms which were made from card, edged with irregular paving slabs cut from thick paper. The sides of each rail were then painted using Humbrol rust colour, the paint being used sparingly to avoid damaging the plastic chairs on the Peco track. Ballast (stone chippings) was then applied carefully to sleeper-top level using an old paintbrush to work it into place. Resin W adhesive, diluted with an equal amount of water plus a few drops of washing-up liquid to reduce surface tension, was then added to the ballast using a medical dropper. When using this technique it is important to use sufficient adhesive to spread throughout the ballast but care must be taken to avoid excess liquid reaching the surface of the chipboard since this will cause the board to swell, leading to uneven track and possible derailments. I observed this effect on an earlier layout where track was laid directly on to chipboard and hence now recommend the use of cork as a barrier layer between the ballasted track and the baseboard surface.

During the ballasting phase provision was made for the mechanical uncouplers developed for the layout and as uncouplers are rarely seen on 009 layouts, a brief description may be of interest (see also Fig 3). A short length of brass tube is mounted through the chipboard at the required location and the uncoupling ramp (thin plastic card) is raised and lowered by means of a small length of rod passing through the tube. A pull wire from the rear of the baseboard activates a crank mechanism mounted beneath the board, a rubber band being used to restore the crank to its normal position. The uncouplers work very reliably once the art of positioning the train accurately has been mastered by the operators.

Scenery and buildings

The basic scenery on 'Milborne' was built using papier-mâché applied to card strips stretching between plywood formers. When the papier-mâché had set, a thin working surface of Polyfilla was added. This was painted with poster colours before the usual scenic dressings were applied, again using Resin W as an adhesive. Road and platform surfaces were painted using matt greys from the Humbrol range. The millstream is made with clear casting resin, which unfortunately took many weeks to set completely, I think as a result of using old materials, since the resin has a short shelf-life.

One aspect of the hobby which gives me considerable pleasure is the construction of buildings and the structures on 'Milborne' are all scratch-built. The buildings were based on thick card shells with stonework represented by Peco Texture Material, scribed with a modelling knife and painted with water-colours. Doors, windows and other details were added, using a mixture of thin card and plastic strip. Embossed plastic card was used for slate roofs, whilst computer punchings were applied individually to represent tiles on the miller's cottage. Gutters and drainpipes were chosen from mouldings in

Fig 3 A section through the uncouplers. The size of the plastic card ramp is 12 mm × 5 mm approximately and the guide wire prevents rotation of the ramp when raised and lowered by the crank mechanism.

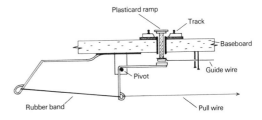

1 A petrol railcar and trailer await departure from Milborne St Giles. The simple plastic card body of the railcar is mounted on a Rivarossi Bo-Bo chassis. Note the inconspicuous uncoupling ramp immediately in front of the railcar.

2 Loco No 7 Sparrowhawk, arriving with a passenger train, passes the goods shed and goods platform. No 7 is a Weald Models kit on a Minitrix 2-6-2 chassis.

3 A view of the station and station building. Note the use of 00-gauge accessories from a variety of manufacturers.

4 Loco No 7 passing the mill. The stonework on the building is represented by Peco Texture Material with individual stones painted with watercolours. The tiles on the millhouse are tiny computer punchings.

5 The petrol railcar about to cross the millstream as it approaches Milborne Station.

the Linka range. The granary has a thatched roof—an initial attempt to represent this using plumbers' hemp resulted in the model bearing an uncanny likeness to a well-known canine character from The Magic Roundabout! With little time to experiment before attending the layout's first exhibition, a reasonable impression of thatch was obtained using Texture Material scribed with an old Stanley Knife blade.

Many hours were spent adding the small details which bring any layout to life. Threading nylon filament through Slaters fence posts and painting 4 mm figures are both excellent therapy after a long day at work! The station fencing was adorned with a liberal supply of enamel advertisements and other details such as gas lamps, name-boards, trolleys, etc, were chosen from the comprehensive stocks of my local model shop. Most of the dirt and grime on the layout has been confined to the loco shed area, although the company's servants have followed the usual practice of leaving old rails, sleepers,

coils of wire, scrap timber, etc, distributed at random throughout railway property! I had intended to use printed skypaper for the back-scene but failed to purchase any in time for the exhibition already mentioned. Fortunately my wife set to work with poster paints and produced a very realistic hazy sky effect which has received favourable comments from a number of fellow enthusiasts.

Taken as a whole the scenery can best be described as idealistic with plenty of green grassy areas and well-maintained buildings with stonework a little over-emphasised. My defence is that model scenery is more analogous to a painting than a photographic image.

Rolling stock

Building the present layout has taken some nine months of fairly intensive work and, until recently, there has been little attempt to build additional rolling stock to supplement that which I possessed at the beginning of the project. Thus many of the photographs show stock from the Liliput range which, although of continental origin, can be recommended as a reliable starting point for newcomers to narrow-gauge modelling. The locomotives on the layout are all named after birds of prey and are painted LNER apple green! Brief details of these are given below. Coaches are painted red and cream.

Locomotives

Hobby/Owl—Playcraft 0-4-0s less cabs and with cut down chimneys. Now used sparingly as they have run many miles on previous layouts.

Falcon—Peco Varikit on a Minitrix 0-6-0 chassis. Reliable and needs little maintenance.

Merlin—Plastic card body on Fleischmann 0-6-0 diesel chassis (second-hand). Reliable but wheels need cleaning before a running session.

Buzzard—Minitrains 0-4-0 Baldwin. Needs frequent cleaning to ensure good running.

Goshawk—Liliput 0-6-2. Reliable but valve gear fell apart on one side. Needs little maintenance.

Sparrowhawk—Weald Models Lynton & Barnstable kit on Minitrix 2-6-2 chassis. Reliable and requires little maintenance.

Railcar—Plastic card body on a Rivarossi BoBo chassis taken from an American diesel 'switcher' purchased cheaply second-hand. Very reliable once surplus oil had been removed!

Future plans

A new rake of coaches, using Ratio Coach sides and mounted on Liliput bogies, is being constructed and the next task will be to build more authentic-looking goods stock. Several N-gauge mechanisms have been acquired and will be used to increase the locomotive stock as time permits. Two further scenic boards are currently planned to feature the village of Milborne St Giles and these will be inserted between the present overbridge and the fiddle-yard bringing the total length of the layout to 15 ft. This part of the project will inevitably proceed slowly because the buildings will all be scratch-built. There is plenty of scope to extend the line further to include the stone quarry and perhaps eventually a second terminus will replace the fiddle-yard.

6 *Loco No 3 stands alongside the coaling stage, the former coach body now used by the permanent way department is shown in the background.*

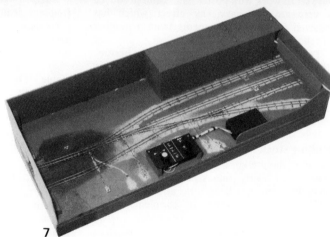

7 *The fiddle yard.*

Narrow-gauge modelling to 009/HOe standards has many followers in the hobby and is certainly one solution for those with limited space available. Satisfying layouts can be built in an area which would be inadequate for standard gauge, but at the same time the modeller can make good use of the wide range of kits and scenic items available for 4 mm scale modelling. For a long while the popular image of narrow gauge modelling has been based on unreliable 'rabbit-warren' type layouts which have all too frequently appeared as space fillers at exhibitions. I hope that 'Milborne' will join the growing number of more serious narrow-gauge layouts which aim to show that 009 and HOe models can be at least as reliable as those of any other gauge. A welcome recent development has been an increase in trade support mainly in the form of locomotive and rolling stock kits. Perhaps one day a British manufacturer will introduce a range of ready-to-run 009 gauge equipment, but here I am probably ending this story in the way it began—in a world of fantasy!

●

Improving ready-to-run locomotives

Chris Ellis

Today's railway modeller enjoys a rich selection of top quality model locomotives at very reasonable prices, with a choice and standard of excellence which did not exist even ten years ago. For, in the last few years, new companies have entered the field and the struggle to capture a good segment of the market by the different manufacturers has led to a general upgrading of standards of finish and detailing. Hence recent models of British locomotives have the sort of detail (such as brake shoes, sand boxes, separate hand rails, etc) that was formerly found only on the leading European makes. In the old days such details as these were usually omitted and the chassis and wheels were themselves often something of a compromise. By today's standards, therefore, some model locos that were being sold just a few years ago now look stark and sometimes even a little crude, and, what is more, some of the 'last generation' of these models remain on sale even now. Most of these remarks apply to the popular scales of N and 00/H0 where the available ranges of models are large, but even the 0 gauge modeller these days has a modest selection of ready-to-run model locomotives to choose from.

What all this amounts to is that the key to a good model railway layout, efficient and realistic motive power, is yours almost without effort. Indeed only your spending money will limit your choice, but even then there are plenty of good locos to be had at quite modest prices as a look at advertisements and catalogues will show. If you are a complete beginner you may not know enough about the prototype locomotive to know whether you are buying a very accurate replica, but in passing it is worth mentioning that the various model railway magazines generally review new releases when they appear, so it is worth seeing what has been written about a particular model before you commit your money. There are lots of key factors to consider, and among them are the following: 1 You may be a beginner with one of the cheaper, simpler 'train set' locomotives. 2 You may have a particular favourite which is only available as one of the older generation of models which lacks modern standards of detail. 3 You may have one of the current generation of models from recent years, highly detailed and of true scale appearance in virtually all respects. 4 You may have one of these modern models—and there are a few—where even the best efforts of the designers have failed to ensure a 100 per cent accurate end product. Sometimes you do not find this out until after you have bought it and there are many instances where the loco may be a particular favourite of yours even if it is a little inaccurate!

Your models might fall into any of these categories but, whatever the position as it applies to you, the one certain thing is that you can have a pleasant time giving your models some added detail and/or individuality. In essence, what has now become known as the 'ready-to-run' locomotive model gives you an excellent replica, available straight from your dealer's shelves, looking most realistic and extremely well made. Put it on the track and it will perform nicely right out of the box. Many model railway enthusiasts do just that, and aside from the recommended maintenance (oiling, brush replacement and so on) they do not think of changing what the model manufacturer supplies. Indeed, this seems to be such a common attitude—accepting a model as purchased—that even the models on many a big exhibition layout look just as though they are straight from the pages of the model manufacturer's catalogue—shiny, sparkling, and carrying the same running number as everybody else's model!

If you recognise your models in this description why not try to do something about it? In the old days modellers got some individuality into their layouts because nearly all locos had to be scratch-built or assembled from kits. Today many more modellers can join in the model railway hobby, simply because so much is available in the 'ready-to-run' category. Ironically enough, this very fact has resulted in a certain 'sameness' from layout to layout because the identical models are seen everywhere. But essentially one important element of the model

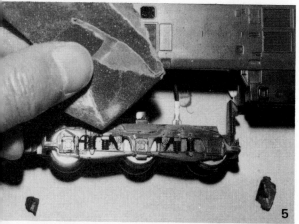

1 *An Airfix-GMR 1400 Class loco getting the individual treatment. In this case it is also being converted slightly to the non-auto fitted 5800 Class. Here the top feed detail is carefully cut away, but the model is otherwise in its 'as purchased' state.*

2 *The tool boxes have been moved further forward and the moulded plastic hand rails on the cab have been carved off and replaced with wire staples. Heat pipes have been added to the buffer beam and the scar on the cab side is due to the removal of an electrical cable not found on the 5800 Class.*

3 *The completed model now has a driver and fireman, etched brass Kings Cross plates, and a fair amount of grime based on a picture of the real No 5800 as in 1948. Note also the lamp iron in front of chimney, the painted hand rails and the painted wheels and side rods.*

4 *Hornby Class 37 diesel as purchased; a popular model of good appearance but wrong or lacking in certain details.*

5 *All the bogie side detail must be removed as most of it is wrong for an actual Class 37. Unwanted sand boxes at the ends are cut away.*

6 *Plastic card is used for new scale length overlays, glued over the existing belly tanks, and new detail is added to the bogie sides from plastic card and scrap plastic.*

railway hobby is its scope for creativeness and imagination. Whatever else you do in the cause of creativity, why not start with the locomotives? You need only basic skills to enhance or slightly alter a ready-to-run model loco to make it quite distinctive for your layout. The only thing likely to vary from model to model is the amount of extra detailing it needs, for the simpler 'train set' locos and older models may need additions, simply to bring them up to latest standards, while some of the most recent models may require only minimal attention.

There are dozens of models available and it is not possible to cover more than a few examples here. But let us assume you get one of the popular modern releases such as the Airfix-GMR GWR 1400 class 0-4-2T tank engine in 00 scale. For a start it comes in GWR or BR finish, and you will have chosen it to suit your

period. It is a great model as it comes and you may think that that is all there is to it. But wait a minute; every other purchaser has one like it, how can your model take on an individual touch? Straight away you are on to that important aspect of the hobby, research. Do not take the model for granted. Get hold of some books which show pictures of the real thing—almost any GWR book has pictures of them, but there are several books dealing with loco classes which have technical details, drawings and many photographs. Study the pictures with the model in front of you, and all sorts of things will come to light.

For a start you will find that the top feed fitting on the boiler was a late addition, and many locos in the class never had it at any time. Before 1946 the number series was 48XX and not 14XX. Also, before 1946, there were no steps on the bunker sides, and at all times there was great variety in the actual placing of the tool boxes alongside the front splasher. Some locos had the auto gear box on the front buffer beam, not the rear as in the model, and there was a whole class numbered in the 58XX series with no auto gear fitted. You will find the GWR version of the model is suitable for the 1946-47 period only and, before that, even the lettering styles differed—usually a GWR circular monogram from 1934-46 and the words 'Great Western' in front. Then all locos had a raised brass number plate, not the flat transfer applied to the model. From all this you can see that there is an immense amount of potential which will enable you to come up with a selected loco of the class which looks appreciably different in detail from the basic model as purchased. Even if you settle for the model as it comes you can buy a pair of etched brass number plates quite cheaply from the Kings Cross range and glue them over the transfers. The model looks better already! But you can go way beyond that. If your layout is to be set in the 1930s period, you will need to do more, such as remove the GWR lettering and replace it with a GWR totem transfer, select 48XX number plates, and saw off the top feed and bunker steps, filing the areas smooth and repainting the areas. It is advisable, where you can, to select an actual loco where more than one photograph is given (the reference books again) and give your model the finish and detailing to suit. Watch those tool boxes on 14XX locos. They may be further forward (or even missing) on certain locos. Where are they on the loco you are modelling? They may need to be sawn off and re-sited.

So much for prototype detail. You should do

7 *Unwanted moulding lines are rubbed down and removed as is the paper 'stick-on' headcode. The front detail is added, including heat and brake pipes, correct lights, screen wipers and new bigger horns. Hand rails made from wire are added at the corners.*

8 *The completed model with all the added detail, and modern 'twin dot' marker lights (from Letraset) replacing the headcode. Extra bogie and front end detail makes a subtle difference to the model.*

this exercise for each and every locomotive you add to your stock. But what about other improvements? Look hard at the 1400 class 0-4-2T and you will find very little actually missing but the steam heat pipes are not supplied, so you need to add one at each end below the buffer beam. Then, again, the various bunker and tank side hand rails are simply moulded into the plastic. The model will look much better with real wire hand rails here so carve off and rub down the moulded rails, drill or burn (with a hot pin) some locating holes, and make actual rails from wire—though for 00-scale models like this one, office staples of the Rexel or Bambi variety are often just right, try them for size or adaptation. Next crunch up a bit of coal (with a hammer—outdoors) and put the small pieces in a polythene bag for safe keeping. Smear glue over the plastic coal and sprinkle your crushed coal over this to give the bunker a realistic load. Add a driver and fireman and the model really starts to look like a working loco, not just a catalogue illustration.

Now all you need to do is to make it look a

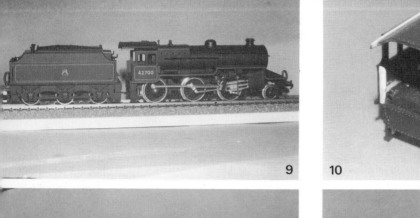

9   *The Lima Crab as purchased looks good but has some dimensional errors.*

10   *The cab and footplate are widened with plastic card. As with all this work, it is useful to have as much pictorial reference material as possible and, for the more complicated work, a scale drawing is useful too.*

11   *The tender body is shortened by cutting a 2 mm strip from the rear end and re-assembling it.*

12   *The correct pattern balance weights are added from plastic card—missing from the model as supplied.*

13   *The completed model has hand rails added on the tender, a driver and fireman, cab glazing, coal on tender top and correct dimensions. AWS equipment was not fitted on this particular loco so it is removed from the model, which is in 'dirty' BR finish of 1956.*

little 'used', for real locomotives, be they steam, diesel, or electric, get quite weathered and dirty with use even if they are cleaned fairly frequently. Start off by painting the bright wheel rims and the centre hubs 'dirty black', then paint the side rods a mix of brownish black. This gives another immediate improvement in looks for it actually makes the wheels look 'finer' in scale. It may be that you prefer your locomotive to be bright and shiny and there is nothing to stop you leaving all your models in an 'ex-works' condition if that is your wish. However, even freshly painted locomotives gather a bit of wear first time out, and this applies to all forms of traction. There is staining and discolouration from exhaust and muck is thrown up from the track, quite apart from runs caused by steam or water on steam locos, grease dribbles, and much else. So long as it is not overdone, a little light work to simulate some of these effects can add greatly to the realism of the model.

Skilled owners of an air brush can do wonders here, but if you run only to ordinary brushes you can still do a reasonable job using the 'dry brush' technique—dip only the tip of the brush in the paint, work out most of the paint on a piece of scrap, then apply the 'dirt' by very light strokes in the required area. You can practise on old discarded models first or on plastic scrap to perfect the technique. If you look at the real thing you will note that 'wear and weathering' dirt is hard to define in terms of colour. You tend to notice the contrast colours, so on a black engine the greyish-brown staining stands out most, while on a light coloured engine the blackish-brown colours show up more. The thing to do is to get a selection of dull matt colours—white, grey, 'track colour', black, brown, 'underframe dirt', and, a useful shade from several paint makers, 'mushroom'. Make a 'palette' from a piece of card, put on a blob of each colour, and use your brush to mix various combinations of shade as required. You may have whitish dribbles from wash-out plugs and cylinder relief valves, brownish dirt round hand rails and along ledges, sooty dirt on footplates and tender tops, and so on. It is useful, again, to study pictures of the real thing and, in the case of diesels and electrics, actually to see them and study them next time you are at a station. Note that fresh steam often makes the tops of the boilers and cab roofs shiny in combination with an oily deposit, and runs of water from tank fillers and oil from fuel fillers also shine. A neat way of simulating these is to use gloss clear varnish applied with a brush, though just a touch of Five Minute Epoxy applied with the

little finger can also do the job realistically. Wash your finger well afterwards.

One last point, often overlooked, is to check how the original was painted as compared to the model. Models often have shiny bare metal hand rails or shiny safety valves, yet the full-size loco probably has these painted to match the body colour. Just touching in these fittings accordingly can make a lot of difference. Buffer beams are another area where the style of painting on the model sometimes differs from the real thing. This is particularly so in the case of diesel locos where there is great variety of style. It is so with diesels and electrics, too, where much attention focuses on the buffer beam. For modern locos have a mass of brake, heating, and MU control pipes, and on most models these are missing. Likewise there are screen wipers and other subtle detail fittings often omitted from models. Adding all these can quite transform the appearance of an otherwise good but unexceptionally detailed ready-to-run model and can, in fact, make a considerable difference to the overall look.

Detail changes and weathering of models do not need to be restricted to British outline. Most of the popular French and German loco types have enormous scope for detail changes and weathering. That bright red of the chassis and running gear of German steam locos, well-known from models, was much less noticeable in real life, for a patina of grime toned it down a lot and sometimes the red was not apparent at all under the brownish grey weathering of the chassis. There were many variations in 'plumbing' on European steam locos, and any given model is usually just representative of the type. If we take Fleischmann's fine DB Class 94 (in H0 or N scales) as an example, the real thing could have had its feed-water heater (and associated piping) in any of three positions (or none at all). There were at least three combinations of bunker and cab styles, at least two styles of marking (according to period), one or two domes on the boiler, and many tiny variations in such matters as positions of foot steps and hand rails. You can make a Fleischmann's model look quite distinctive by finding pictures of real locos, selecting an actual machine, and making your model look like it. This can be repeated for virtually every loco, though some, like Roco's Class 23 or Liliput's Class 42 (being very recent models) are so highly detailed (even including a few alternative detail parts with the model) that they need little more than weathering and the addition of coal in the tender.

14

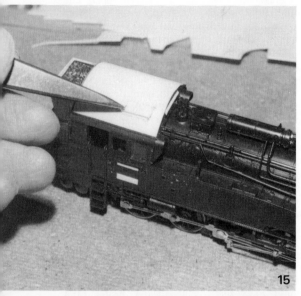

15

16

Certain models come with errors of omission or dimension, and these may need more work. A lot of British outline models lack front steps because they would either be difficult to mould in mass production or would hinder the bogie swing on tight curves. You can make these from plastic card, or can take them from kits in some cases (such as the Airfix unmotorised 00 loco kits), or buy them as spare castings from specialist suppliers. Similarly cylinders may be too short, glazing omitted from cabs, or brake shoes and sand boxes left off altogether. A favourite omission is sand pipes—the sand box is there but not the pipe to the wheel rim. Micro-rod or wire can remedy the omission but it is important with sand boxes or brake shoes to ensure that none of these additions catch on the running gear or jam the wheels. If in doubt, leave this area alone. Another problem, mainly with British models, is an unsightly and unprototypical gap of daylight between front footplate and bogie, again to allow for bogie swing on tight curves. This can be overcome visually by cementing black plastic card strips, cut to clear the wheels, under the front footplate in line with the main frames.

A few models have other errors such as a footplate which is too long, a tender which is too long, or even a footplate which is too narrow. These need more work on them, some addition of plastic card, and a little cutting and amending. Taking two popular examples at random, the Hornby 'Hall' class loco needs to have the front end of the footplate cut off, slightly shortened, and re-cemented in place with a deeper buffer beam as well to improve its appearance greatly. Aside from this, the cutting away of the moulded plastic nameplate, the addition of real wire hand rails to replace moulded ones, and the addition of chassis detail will really transform it into a showpiece. The Lima 'Crab' is a nice model which is too narrow and has its tender too long, so it is necessary to cut off the cab sides, insert plastic card strips to widen it, and then glue plastic card to the footplate sides, widening the whole model by about 3 mm. It takes longer than just the basic detailing of other models, but the end result is well worth it.   ●

14 *A Fleischmann HO DB Class 94 locomotive as purchased.*
15 *The detail variations on this one include a different style of cab roof and bunker, added number plates and a rain strip on the cab front, all made from plastic card.*
16 *The completed model, very dirty, with weather screens over the doors, and with added crew.*

A Class 13 locomotive

Ralph Fenwick

To provide more powerful units for shunting, diesel locomotives are sometimes coupled in pairs and converted for 'master and slave' or, as it is known in the United States, 'cow and calf' working. The cab is removed from the slave or calf and the two locomotives are then operated together as a single unit from the cab of the master or cow unit. Thus only one driver is required.

In the United States, Electro-Motive (EMD) have built units of this type for many different railroads. They were designed for use as switchers, often for hump yards, but have occasionally been employed for road service. For the modeller of American prototype, Athearn make ready-to-run models of the EMD SW 1,500 hp Bo-Bo switcher cow and calf units in nine different liveries and these models are available in this country from Victors of Islington.

In Britain 'master and slave' operation is very uncommon. A.J. Booth in his excellent book *A Pictorial Survey of Standard Gauge Industrial Diesels Around Britain* (published by D. Bradford Barton Limited) includes an illustration of one of several pairs of Brush/Bagnall diesel electric 0-4-0s worked as 'master and slave' units at the Margam Steelworks and also mentions that, at the British Steel Corporation's Cleveland Steelworks, Thomas Hill (Rotherham) Ltd locomotives are operated in this way.

The only British Rail 'master and slave' locomotives are the Class 13 units used for hump shunting in the Tinsley Marshalling Yard at Sheffield. These three 700 hp 0-6-0 + 0-6-0 diesel electric locomotives were produced in 1965 from six Class 08s with 110 volt auxiliaries. The master and slave locomotives are permanently coupled and the cabs of the latter have been removed. Extra weight has been added to the units.

Though I have not had the opportunity to see these units I was intrigued by photographs of them and decided that a model of one would be an interesting and unusual addition to my locomotive roster. It seemed convenient and

logical to follow the prototype example and to convert two 08 Class models. Several models of this class are, or have been, produced by firms including Triang, Wrenn, Hornby and Lima (the almost identical 09). Inspection showed that with some of these I would have to take out the motor to enable the cab to be cut away in the manner of the prototype conversion. If I had been able to obtain a cheap second-hand model, perhaps damaged or non-working, I would have been happy to do this but as I could not and was going to have to buy new model 08s it seemed a shame to have to remove the motor of one of them. I therefore decided on the Hornby model in which the motor does not extend into the cab (R 354 in the current catalogue). Thus both units remain motorised, making the combination more powerful. Because this model requires two locomotives it may seem a rather extravagant project. However I was able to obtain the two 08s from one of the larger mail order dealers for about £16 so the completed model is not unduly expensive considering that it is a fairly impressive unit because of its size and rarity. In addition I can always run the master locomotive as an ordinary Class 08 when I wish.

The modifications to the slave body are straightforward but care is advisable as any mistakes or accidental damage could prove expensive! I cut off the top half of the cab with horizontal and vertical cuts with a razor saw along the lines shown on the side view picture, leaving a little excess to be filed away rather than risking cutting too much off with the saw. The remaining parts of the cab doors were then removed, using the saw and a modelling knife, down to floor level. A floor section, 19 mm × 30 mm, was cut from 60 thou thick plastic card to fit against the inner faces of the sides and back of the cab and was cemented into place. I then blocked off the open end of the body where the cab had been cut away with a piece of 30 thou thick plastic card. This was cut slightly oversize at the top and was then filed and sanded down to exact size after it was fixed in position. A further piece of 60 thou thick plastic card was cut to fit across the cab immediately in front of

1 *The Hornby 00-gauge 0-6-0 diesel shunter which is in BR Green livery. Two of these models are required for this conversion project.*

2 *On this side view of the Hornby model the section of the body to be cut away for the slave unit is shown shaded.*

3 *The locomotive body—after the initial vertical and horizontal saw cuts have been made to remove the upper part of the cab.*

4 *The next step is to cut out the remaining parts of the cab doors.*

5 *The cab floor of black 60 thou thick plastic card has been installed and white 30 thou thick plastic card has been used to close off the cut end of the body.*

6 *Additional pieces of plastic card have been cut to fit across between the cab sides, just in front of the door openings, and to fill in the gap between this piece and the body.*

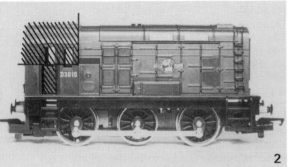

7

7 *The only modification to the chassis which is required is to cut off the cab end coupling counterweight. This picture shows an unaltered chassis at the rear while the chassis in front has been modified for use in the slave unit.*

8

8 *The completed slave unit after removal of the numbers and logos and after painting.*

the doorways, coming up to the level of the horizontal cut across the cab. Additional pieces of thinner plastic card, cut to fit by trial and error, were cemented in place to fill in the gaps between this cross piece and the body, sloping as shown in the photographs. Small pieces of thin plastic card were also fitted in to the remaining lower parts of the cab windows to fill them in. Any cracks and gaps were then filled in with Humbrol Customizing Body Putty. When set hard the whole area was filed and sanded smooth. This completes the modifications required apart from painting. I decided to retain the BR Green finish of the Hornby models and touched up the parts fabricated from plastic card to match. The numbers and BR logos on the slave unit are scraped carefully off and these areas are also touched up with paint. The

numbers on the master unit should really be changed to an appropriate one such as D 4500 but I have not replaced the ones on my model as I want to run it as a separate 08 Class locomotive as well. The model will be enhanced by the addition of the yellow visibility stripes at the front and rear but, unless you can apply these neatly, they are probably better omitted. As an alternative to the older green livery the model can be completely repainted in the later BR Blue livery. Double arrow logos and numbers (13 001, 13 002 or 13 003) are available in the SMS transfers range. Again yellow stripes can be applied to both ends of the master and to the front end (but not the cab end) of the slave unit. As I write this I have just heard that Hornby are to issue their 08 Class in BR Blue livery complete with the yellow visibility stripes and this will

9 *The completed master and slave units which make up the Class 13 model.*

10 *A prototype Class 13 locomotive, No 13 002, in operation at Tinsley Yard, Sheffield* (Diesels Nationwide, Oxford Publishing Co).

obviously simplify the production of a Class 13 in the modern livery.

I am very grateful to the Oxford Publishing Co for permission to reproduce the accompanying photograph of the prototype Class 13 locomotive 13 002 at work in the Tinsley Yard, Sheffield in 1976. The photograph is from the book *Diesels Nationwide* by Keith Montague. Photographs of Class 13 units also appear in two books from the Transport Topic Series also published by the Oxford Publishing Co, *No.4 BR Shunters* by C.W. Judge, and *No.10 Spotters Guide to Diesel Recognition* by B. Nicolle. These two latter books also include scale drawings of the Class 13 units. All three books are recommended to diesel modellers. ●

Coaching stock

Richard Gardner

Not so very long ago the 00 modeller had little choice with regard to the type of coaching stock to run on the layout. The keener individuals had the wider range of stock available from the specialist kit manufacturers, but even here the range was somewhat limited by financial constraints. Now the situation is completely changed, for there is a vast range on the market in ready-to-run form at very low prices for the quality, detail, and smooth running performance. The problem is more 'what to buy' rather than one of availability. For the older enthusiast the recent growth in the hobby has brought forth a veritable beanfeast of delightful models. It is only the size of layout and depth of the pocket that limits the possibilities for reproducing reasonably authentic trains from the major railway companies and, of course, British Railways.

In the model press one often sees very nice layouts spoilt by the incorrect mixing of locomotives and coaching stock representing conflicting periods. Although it now seems a long time ago, Hornby offered the LMS, SR and GWR modeller suitably painted BR Mk 1 coaches throughout the late 1960s and most of the 70s. During this span thousands of young modellers happily ran their period expresses with these comparatively modern coaches but this is no longer necessary, thanks to the level of competition between the major producers Hornby, Airfix, Mainline and Lima.

So how do we decide on our coaching stock needs? The various catalogues bulge with different coaches and it is at first a little confusing to look at them all. Perhaps the best way to start is to mimic the full size operators and examine what sort of traffic you are handling on your layout. Instead of selecting coaches for looks alone, go for those which will complement your locomotives and be of lasting use. The luxury stock can come later.

Let us go through the ready-to-run coaching stock availability lists to see what is needed for the likely services to be run on the average layout. It is quite possible that the models shown in the table will be supplemented by additions to the range over the years and others may be withdrawn.

1 *The current standard of British ready-to-run 00-scale coaches. This model is a Stanier brake 2nd repainted and relined from an LMS model. The lining is a black ink ruled line on a wider yellow band and the badge is from the Kemco range. The number is yet to be added.*

Coaching stock from the major ready-to-run firms

	GWR	LMS	LNER	SR	BR
Branch line	Autocoach A	Sub comp A			Sub Comp A, Sub bk A
	B Set A	Sub bk A			Autocoach, B set A
and Local	Railcar L				WR Railcar L
	4 Wheel H				DMU L
Semi-fast	Coach H	Coach H	Coach H	Coach H	Stanier comp H
or Express	Bk H	Bk H	Bk H	Bk H	Stanier bk H
	Restaurant H	Comp A	Sleeper H	Comp A	Stanier comp A
	Centenary A	Bk A		Bk A	Stanier bk A
	Centenary bk A	Open 3rd A			Centenary A
		Rest A			Centenary bk A
		Panelled M			Open 3rd A
		Pan bk M			Rest A
					Bulleid comp A
					Bulleid bk A
					Panelled comp M
					Panelled bk M
					Mk 1 Comp L M
					Mk 1 bk L M
					Mk 1 2nd L M
					Mk 1 Buffet H L M
					Mk 1 Full bk L
					Mk 2A series H
					Mk 2B series L
					Mk 2D series A
					Mk 3 series H & J

Luxury trains
Pullman coach H   W   BR   HST   H
Pullman brake H   W   BR   APT   H
In addition to the above authentic models there are various 'typical' corridor and suburban coaches produced by Graham Farish in company colours and BR maroon.

Symbols
A   Airfix,   H   Hornby,   M   Mainline,   L   Lima,   J   Jouef.

It can be seen from the chart that there are a very large number of coaches available. If you model the modern British Rail scene then just about every type of coach can be bought for locomotive-hauled trains. Next best off are LMS modellers with the GWR close behind. It should be remembered that coaches wandered far from their home companies and regions and so just because you have built a GWR branch it does not mean that you are automatically limited to using only GWR coaching stock. Although Southern coaches tended to keep within regional boundaries more than the others, the cross country express could take through coaches 'from one end of the land to the other.

The majority of model railway layouts do not have the space to take scale-length trains. Even the largest club layouts often have to make compromises to enable long trains to fit into the track plan. This is why the branch line or secondary route is so popular for the average layout. If shorter trains are run they look far better and can fit the run-around loops and platforms. It is a common mistake for newcomers to the hobby to try and emulate the full-size main line railway with 10- or 12-coach trains buzzing around a limited oval, tail-chasing at its worst! If space is at a premium then the local trains should be restricted and the whole layout run along reduced lines. If modelling the GWR then a one- or two-coach autocar plus push-pull loco, or perhaps a two-coach B set, would be ideal. Those favouring the BR scene could use a railcar set or a loco-hauled two- or three-car train.

Although specialised suburban stock is available for local trains it should be pointed out that main line stock can be used for the shortest

2 *A full size preserved Stanier brake 3rd, of a slightly different design to the Airfix model, at Highley on the Severn Valley Railway.*

3 *This Collett open 3rd was built for summer holiday traffic on the GWR in 1937. It is important not to muddle periods when modelling pre-nationalisation railways. Reference books are vital to get the correct stock to complement locomotives.*

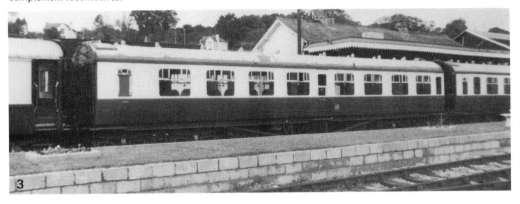

trains as well. If you look through the many photo-albums of trains through the ages, you will see plenty of locals being run with older main line stock. The express coach of one year could find itself relegated to a relative backwater in a very short time — and might then move back to the main line. Even today BR Mk 1 coaches can be found on certain low-density routes running in ones and twos behind such locos as the Class 25 diesels. Modern air-conditioned coaches do not work the small lines in this way yet but the Mk 1s and a few early Mk 2s can often be noted on very obscure-looking trains.

As so much stock is so readily available there is little excuse for running unrepresentative trains. Let us consider the make up of a few typical train formations. We should aim to provide the same balance of capacity as on the real railways. There should be adequate second (or third) class capacity with some first class seating and a guard's brake coach with luggage space. It can vary between trains but generally the first class accommodation is minimal on local trains whereas on inter-city trains it is often almost half the total. A cross-country, semi-fast, loco-hauled train could have the following coaches: brake second, composite first/second, all-second and brake second; or brake second, all-second, brake composite; or all-second, all second, composite, brake second. For refreshments on the train a buffet car would be more appropriate than a full restaurant/kitchen car, which would look better on a longer train. What should be avoided is a train composed entirely of composite or first class coaches — unless it is supposed to be a special working. A train without first class seating is more common,

4 *This GW composite brake coach is preserved in pristine condition on the Severn Valley Railway.*

5 *There are many preserved Pullman cars surviving. This one is at Steamtown, Carnforth. Pullmans were attached to ordinary trains on special occasions as well as running in complete sets.*

6 *The Lima full-brake is made to fit the standard Lima underframe common to BR Mk 1 coaches but is over-length for this particular vehicle. This model has been repainted and relined with the window edges painted matt black to reduce the apparent thickness of the plastic moulded sides.*

especially in holiday areas, but the aim should be a realistic balance.

The brake coaches are usually at the front or rear of the train — or at both ends on slightly longer formations. If some of the wayside stations have short platforms then a brake coach might be positioned in the middle so as to be sure that luggage can be unloaded easily without the appropriate coach over-running the platform ends. Again, it is worth studying the photographs of the real thing to see what formations equate to your own needs.

Very few home layouts can comfortably take more than five scale-length coaches in a train without becoming unwieldy. Apart from the problem of fitting such a train into the station platforms without fouling points, the question of accommodation in the 'fiddle yard' or carriage sidings becomes an important point. Most real stations can 'swallow-up' a five-coach train with plenty of space at either end of the platform. Allowing for an all-round scaling-down to achieve realism in miniature, one finds that local trains of two or three coaches look right and expresses of five coaches are quite visually acceptable.

The main line coaches made by Hornby Dublo, Tri-ang and Trix were slightly under-

scale in length but did not look so bad when on the layout. Now that Mk 1 coaches are the correct length they tend to look too big for most layouts! The 75 ft Mk 3 coaches are monsters by earlier standards and the dead scale Jouef models look superb sandwiched between a pair of Hornby HST power vehicles on a big club layout. However, the Hornby Mk 3s, which are a compartment short in comparison, nevertheless look right and save space on the average layout.

Having selected our coaches we now need to make them look more realistic. It is most important not to overdo the weathering or you may destroy the intricate lettering and paint finish of the sides. The sides of the coaches can be left alone and attention given to the roof, ends and underframe, including the bogies. The roof soon gets weathered down to a dark-grey/matt black in service and so white, silver or light grey roofs can be repainted. Ends and under-floor areas should be a grimy brown/matt black colour and this can be achieved by careful dry brushing with dark earth colour oils. Try and pick out the details which are often lost to view when the model is left with glossy black under-frames. Wheel rims can be painted white when ex-works but in service dull down and so look

better if repainted a metallic black.

Small details can be added to give the models a more delicate look if they are not going to be handled by youngsters. Typical additions can be vacuum and steam heating pipes, footboards, wire handrails and roof destination boards. Some modellers semi-permanently couple groups of coaches (or rakes) with corridor connections in contact with each other and close-fitting couplings with scale distances between each vehicle. This depends on your curves. If you have the standard set-track curves then close coupling is not practical. You need curves of 40 in radius or even larger to avoid buffer and corridor lock on reverse curves.

Adding more variety is the option of repainting ready-to-run stock in different schemes. Although most of the models are sold in two alternate liveries it may be that you can modify them further to suit your own layout. To take two examples — the Hornby Gresley coaches are very nice in simulated varnished teak but could be given carmine and cream livery for the 1950s era or lined maroon for the 1957-67 period. The Airfix Stanier coaches can also be repainted to the familiar BR lined maroon. Numbering is available in the Kemco range as

waterslide transfers, or the slightly more delicate PC range, which is not so easy to apply until one has mastered the special technique.

Moving on from ready-to-run models one comes on to the various kits. A really vast range is now available ranging from the Ratio plastic kits of early pre-grouping stock to the MTK range which covers virtually every BR coach as well as a good many earlier coaches. The completion of the kits depends very much on the skill of the builder. The metal kits are expensive and usually bogies, couplings and wheels have to be bought separately. Apart from those offering pre-printed sides, such as MAJ and PC, the builder must carry out all the tricky painting and lining himself. A comprehensive reference library is also needed as some of the instructions can be rather spartan. Before tacking a complex coach kit the beginner would do well to discuss what is required with someone experienced in model construction, or with the man in the local specialist model shop. There is a lot more to operating realistic model passenger trains than simply buying the first coach that happens to look nice in the catalogue. With a little thought, however, there is no excuse for not getting it right. There has never been a better time for the model railway enthusiast.   ●

Detailing and building coaching stock

E.R.H. Francis

In another article in this book the different kinds of coaching stock required for different layouts are discussed, but what does one do if the stock one requires is not readily available? The obvious answer is to build it oneself, but this may have its drawbacks. It takes time and experience to hand-build good coaching stock, but there are ways of making it simpler. If one requires really unusual vehicles, then they will have to be hand-built, either by oneself or by a professional modelmaker. If, however, the demands are not too exotic, then there may be kits available, and sometimes the ready-to-run products of the larger manufacturers can be adapted.

Taking the last first, this is a good way to start as the basic structure has been provided and all one has to do is add the details and alter the livery as required. Although some of the older manufacturers' products can never be more than toys, as they are basically not scaled down from the original, many of the newer products are accurate in as far as they go and are a good basis for an excellent model. The experience gained in detailing these is invaluable when building by hand.

The Airfix Auto-coach is very sound in as far as it does go, and deserves to have the improvements done to it which, if done by the manufacturer, would add too much to the cost of production and would limit the market, which would in turn increase the price even more. Lest anyone thinks this is going to be biased towards the Great Western Railway, this is only taking a specific item to illustrate a general principle that can be applied to stock for any company. The largest market is for the GWR, and these days manufacturers have to be sure of a quick and sure return on their high development costs on any new item.

Several manufacturers produce stock for the older companies, and, for the reasons mentioned before, cannot produce in every livery that a vehicle carried during a long life. A lot can be done just by repainting and surface detailing. If such items as door handle mouldings are removed and brass ones substituted, repainting will be essential. So, let us examine the Auto-coach and see what can be done with it; it is an extreme case and any others will be a lot easier.

First, it must be decided if the model is to be repainted (if the handles are removed, there will be gaps in the paintwork and the white plastic will show through). If not, then the handles can just be picked out in paint; even this is an improvement. Otherwise, if wire ones are to be substituted, then the mouldings should be cut off with a sharp modelling knife. For the next stages the coach must be taken apart; undo all the screws and carefully prise the other sections apart—most of it just snaps together for easy assembly.

Some basic tools are needed; a sharp modelling knife with spare blades, a couple of needle files, and some small drill bits which can be held in a small pin vice. The lamp-irons and other details should be made out of brass or nickel silver wire and strip or bought as detailing accessories and fitted. The droplight frames should be painted mahogany while the glazing is removed. The Auto-coaches had bars inside the droplights to prevent headless passengers; these should be fitted on the inside of the glazing. The interior should be painted, and any passengers and their luggage fitted. The cab details, which are quite conspicuous, should be painted and fixed; these come from the Dart Castings Detail Kit for this model. Most of the parts required for detailing coaches can be bought from such firms as Dart, ABS, and MAJ. The underframe needs to have the rudimentary battery boxes and other fittings removed, by carefully whittling away with a sharp knife, and replaced by more detailed cast metal ones placed the correct distance behind the solebars and truss rods. The rather delicate corner steps and control rod detail is added, and a slot cut for the screw coupling hook. The underframe is then painted black. Easy!

The body should be re-assembled, painted, lined and lettered. Pressfix sheets give the correct lettering for GWR Auto-coaches, and their lining sheet can be used for the lining. Then

1 *Removing grab handles from a K's kit.*

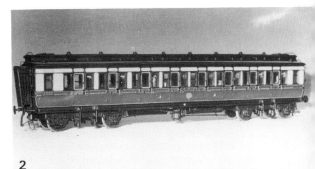

2 *A hand-built GWR clerestory composite.*

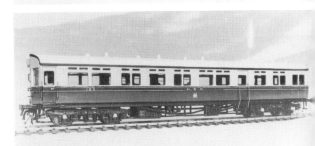

3 *An Airfix auto-coach showing details.*

4 *An Airfix Centenerary showing details.*

the handles should be added; it makes lining easier if this is left until almost last. Then the whole should be given a coat of satin varnish. The Centenary coach illustrated was treated similarly, with the addition of curtains to the windows (castings) and changing the bogies to the correct pressed steel kind; these last can be obtained from MAJ.

The next stage is the use of kits. Some of these are good, some bad; some easy and some only for the more experienced modeller. The more difficult do not necessarily give the best results, and some of the easiest are the best; they often need little more work to make than is involved in detailing a ready-to-run model. Examples of this type are the kits from Ratio and K's. They do need hand painting, but they can be done in various liveries as most are 19th or early 20th century vehicles which often lasted until the 1930s or later. Good as they are, these kits can be easily improved upon in the same way as the stock previously described. As before, the door handles are worth removing and brass ones put in their place. One tip, however, if you are wary of doing this, is to wait until the paint is thoroughly dry—a week or so—and pick the handles out in gold leaf. This gives a far better effect than brass paint. Lamp-irons, jewelled tail lamps, couplings and other details by the specialist manufacturers are available from good model shops.

From these, the next step is the cast or etched brass kit. Casting is fine for small highly detailed models, especially with modern wheels with pin-point axles running in brass bearings, but white-metal is too heavy for a large vehicle. Etched brass is fine if the artwork and etching are good and the design is well thought out from the modeller's viewpoint as well as the manu-facturer's. Some of the most successful designs are those which use a mixture of etching and casting. Cast kits can be assembled using adhesives, but brass really requires soldering and so this method of construction is only for those who have mastered this technique. Most of these kits are supplied with etched sides, ends, floor, and some underframe detail, with the smaller or more solid fittings cast in whitemetal and the roof in plastic—usually vacuum formed. Once the shell has been assembled, the interior detail has to be made up and the model painted. This method does allow the portrayal of wooden panelled stock without needing production runs into the thousands and so vehicles can be produced which are of more specialist interest.

An alternative is the type of kit similar to those produced by MAJ Models of Tiverton, which are mainly plastic; a shell is made up, complete with glazing, and a screen printed overlay is positioned over the sides. This has many advantages; there is a minimum of painting, little or no soldering is required, the plastic is easily worked and assembled, and a pleasing model easily results. Another kind of kit uses pre-cut and formed aluminium sides, with cast ends. This simplifies some work, but they still require more detailing than the plastic kits.

Once you have run out of the vehicles you want that are supplied ready-made or as kits, the only way is to hand-build. If you have success-fully gone through the previous stages, this should present no great difficulty. Styrene sheet, sold as Plastikard, is one of the easiest materials to work in, as it cuts and files very cleanly and gives no problem when painting. So, rather than take any particular model, let us go through the basic stages of a typical coach produced in the 1930s; anything more elaborate is just an extension of this principle. Taking a sheet of .020 in styrene, the basic shape and windows are marked out, cut out with a sharp pointed knife, and filed smooth. Most coaches had a tumble-home, the sides curving in towards the floor. This is produced by placing the edge of the side against the bevel of a ruler and stroking with a rounded blunt instrument. The ends are cut from .060 in styrene. If the coach has a bow end then make this a false end and add the real bowed end of thinner sheet. The floor is cut

from .060 in sheet, and the whole assembled with solvent.

The cantrails are cut from a thin strip of styrene and stretched along the tops of the sides. Droplights can be cut from .005 in sheet or paper, and fixed in place. Glazing is done by cutting thin picture glass into strips; this has the advantage that it does not scratch and it helps to keep the side rigid. It is worthwhile buying a diamond cutter and doing it oneself, although glaziers will do it at a price. Any bars behind the glazing can be ruled on in black paint, but the handrails in the corridors should be plastic rod.

Partitions and screens are from .020 in sheet, and painted after fitting. BSL produce plastic seats which are a good general representation, and the spaces above filled with pictures, maps, mirrors, advertisements, or nothing at all, as was sometimes the case. Carpets and curtains should be fitted, cut from thin cloth or commercial products used; then, if the model is to be shown running in service, add the passengers, not forgetting their clutter such as trunks, cases, baskets, newspapers and magazines.

Roof sections can be bought for some companies from MAJ Models, or they can be made from plastic sheet by gently warming over a wooden former. Gresley and Hawksworth roofs are a problem, and the answer lies in much care and patience. The underframe can be made from styrene strip or brass, or a mixture of both, and the rest of the detailing is as before.

Before the use of steel panelling, mouldings were used to cover the joins in the wooden panels and these were often made quite decorative and gave a company style. For this, one starts with the middle layer, cutting it out like a piece of lace, and laying it on to the main side. When the solvent has dried, cut out the windows and droplights, then the window surrounds. Very often glass was put in from the outside, and held in place by wooden frames called bolections; in this case place a blank over the window, the size of the outside of the bolection, and run solvent into the join. When dry, cut out the central part and cut and file to shape.

Everyone has their own idea of painting, and a lot depends on the materials; modern paints are designed to flow on evenly and dry flat leaving no brushmarks. Used as intended they will be good enough for most purposes; do not try to 'work' the paint, there just isn't room on a small model; always try to finish off with a fine varnish as this protects paint, transfers and bright metal. ●

Three simple coach conversions

John East

This article outlines the construction of two coaches of LMS origin of interest to modellers of the 1950s era. They are constructed from two Hornby Caledonian composite corridor coaches, which appeared in various guises at different times (eg, Southern, LMS) and can often be obtained cheaply second-hand. The major modifications are to the coach sides; the two corridor sides are combined to make a cafeteria car, and the two compartment sides— a lavatory composite non-corridor coach.

Cafeteria car

A number of varieties of these existed at one time, although this is not an exact model of any of them. They were rebuilt from redundant vehicles after World War 2 and became the fore-runners of today's buffet cars.

Use one of the underframes, complete with bogies and ends, and one roof, as they are. Carefully look at one side. The centre door should be retained, but the two on either side are to be removed. The pillars on either side of the window of the upper part of the door can be removed with a fine saw, thus making another large window. The raised 'beading' which represents the rest of the door can be carefully removed with a sharp scalpel.

The two small windows at the extreme ends of the coach need to be converted to doors. Score the edges of the door—the handles and grab rails can be represented by blobs of polystyrene cement applied with a pin point. Fill in with plastic card the two small windows on either side of the central door.

The other side is modified in the same way except that the two large windows on either side of the central door should be filled in. Assemble the sides on to the underframe and secure in place with a few small blobs of glue. At this stage an interior should be fitted if required, but first install a floor cut from plastic card. I constructed a (serving) bar running along the centre portion of the coach (in front of the 'blanked off' large windows) — the central door on this side should have an opaque window made of white plastic card. Tables and chairs are provided at each end of the coach under the windows (construct these from plastic card). Window grab rails are provided only opposite the bar.

I glued the roof in place rather than use the bolts provided because they are unsightly, but this does make it difficult to remove. The coach is finished in the once familiar 'blood and custard' livery, with CAFETERIA written in white (I used Letraset 8pt Futura Bold).

Composite non-corridor

This is a not so common variant which incorporates a lavatory accessible from adjacent compartments. Both sides need to be cut into

1 *The completed cafeteria car model.*

2 *The composite non corridor—side 1.*

3 *The composite non corridor—side 2.*

4 *The end view of the composite non corridor coach showing the hand rail and steps.*

5 A camping coach at a Welsh country station.

several sections. Start at the left-hand end of one side and cut with a razor saw at 16, 148 and 238 mm from this end. This will give you a section of five compartments, one of three compartments, and two short sections containing a small lavatory window. Reassemble with one of the short sections between the two compartment sections, the five compartment section being on your left. Use strips of plastic card to strengthen the joints. The total length of the reconstructed side should be 235 mm (side 1).

The beading will not match up but this does not matter since coaches were often repaired with plain metal sheets, the beading not being replaced. Remove some of the other beading at random so that the joint areas do not stand out. The beading lower on the coach side was more often missing, presumably because the lower panels were more likely to rot due to standing in rain water.

The other side (side 2) is treated similarly, making cuts at 17, 90, 148 and 240 mm from the left-hand end. To reassemble, start with the three compartment section (first class wider door spacings) at the left-hand end. Glue the shorter of the lavatory window sections to this, then the two compartment section and, finally, the other three compartment section. The doors on opposite sides should all be opposite each other. The underframe needs to be shortened to 235 mm by cutting a section out of the middle; likewise the roof, to 240 mm.

Having joined the two halves of the underframe, I provided new frame members just slightly inset from the outer edge of the under-frame, and a cut down battery box, supported by these members, on one side only. Assemble the sides on to the underframe. Cut two ends from plastic card, these should fit over the sides (ie full width of vehicle) but under the roof, and also cover the underframe ends. Score lightly to represent the vertical planks (2.5 mm wide). Fix

a handrail on the left-hand side, curving round beneath the roof, and glue on four steps made from plastic card. Fix buffers in place. Before glueing roof in place, cut some compartment dividers and insert; I did not bother with seats since their absence is not really noticeable through the begrimed small windows. Fill in any gaps with body filler before painting. (The sides are maroon).

A camping coach

Have you a coach which does not run well? Or one which is not up to the standard of your other models in finish or detail? Instead of discarding it or putting it into your scrap box why not make it into a camping coach? The LNER was the first railway company in Britain to use old coaches adapted for use as holiday accommodation which were placed on sidings at country stations in 1933. The other railways later copied the idea and, though the scheme was stopped during the war, British Rail has since reintroduced camping coaches and they are still in use today.

Such a feature is easily modelled and will add interest to a country station or halt on your layout. Any model of one of the older types of coaches can be used. Wooden access steps can be made from card or plastic card and the words 'Camping Coach' applied with dry print lettering. Wooden chocks for the wheels and sleepers across the rails prevent any movement of the coach. Sometimes the track between the points of the siding and the coach is lifted, thus avoiding any risk of rolling stock being shunted against the coach, so that you need not use a siding on your layout but can merely add a short length of track beside the line to accommodate your model camping coach. A gas cylinder beneath the coach provides fuel for cooking and lighting. ●

Inexpensive freight stock in 00 gauge

Andy Brocklebank

For those who prefer to buy their model railways 'out of the box' there are two problems when it comes to freight vehicles—firstly the price (a Hornby 4-wheeled coal truck for example, costs about £1.30), secondly, the 'sameness' of much of the stock. Both of these problems can be avoided quite easily with a small knowledge of the market and this article is intended to introduce a few ideas. It is by no means an exhaustive list, but it is hoped that readers will be encouraged to develop their own thoughts.

The most obvious place to start is in the area of kits. The Airfix range is an excellent choice for modellers of the 1950s and 1960s. Although not a modern image man myself, ('50s and 60s modern?', say my teenage daughters!) I must confess that one of the most exquisite minimum space layouts I have ever seen was a model of an oil terminal with a class 08 diesel and a rake of Airfix Esso tank wagons. Airfix also market kits for a mineral wagon, a meat van, a cattle wagon and a standard BR brake van, at 60p or 70p each.

More traditional freight wagon kits are marketed by various other firms, of which K's, Ratio, Ian Kirk and Coopercraft spring immediately to mind as reasonably priced—from about 90p for a 4-wheeled coal truck to about £1.20 for a van and proportionately more for long-wheelbase and bogie wagons. Of course, these are the plastic ranges—but if you're prepared to spend £4 to £6 on an etched brass kit you shouldn't be reading this!

Once you have tackled a few kits you may well, as I did, get the urge to experiment a bit and try something a little different. If you do, you are making the first steps towards joining kit-bashers anonymous! You can go as far as you like with this, from minor detail differences to the verge of scratch-building. Personally, I have so far always retained the underframe, albeit somewhat modified, as this is the most difficult part of most vehicles to make. I do not propose in this article to go into depth as to methods as two of the other contributors to this book have described in detail examples of such conversions. The model railway magazines also have many drawings as well as suggested modifications and there is a plethora of literature with pictures and drawings to inspire you.

The cheapest way I have found to make a colourful train of private owner coal wagons is to use the Collett card kit range. These are purely body kits and an underframe kit is necessary to complete them. I managed to buy a job lot of Peco underframe kits (these are sprung and have sprung buffers too) at 40p each but, failing that, good old Airfix kits will do as well. They are a little more expensive but you can employ parts from the unused bodies for other projects. The Collett kits, marketed by W & H Models, cost about 35p per card, each card having three or four wagons on it.

Card, of course, is not a very satisfactory medium in itself, but the answer is to reinforce it with plastic card. My method is to cut out the card parts with a sharp craft knife, then place the cut-outs on a sheet of plastic card which has been liberally covered with liquid styrene cement. Press down and leave for an hour or so to set hard. Then cut round the card through the plastic card. The card adheres firmly to the plastic backing. Another tip is to paint all the edges before assembly and thus avoid white strips showing. To complete these models, paint the inside of the wagons matt black and add real coal, crushed to 4 mm scale size lumps. Personally, I glue the coal lumps to a rectangle of plastic card (or use a spare Airfix mineral wagon insert) which I can lift out so as to be able to run coal empties.

The final source of inexpensive wagons I would like to mention is the second-hand market. While buying second-hand locos can be a little hazardous, unless you use a reliable dealer, there's not a lot to go wrong with a four-wheeled wagon. Beware of one thing, however—early Hornby-Dublo and Trix 3-rail stock had uninsulated wheels which will need replacing. Mind you, most people would want to replace scale 2 foot wide wheels anyway! I have used the body parts of Triang and Hornby-Dublo wagons in this way, mounted on Peco or

1, 2, 3 Examples of kit-built models. 1 20-ton 'Toad' GWR brake van (Ratio); GWR 'Mogo' van (Ratio) and GWR 'Parto' van (Ratio). 2 GWR 'Mink D' (Ian Kirk) and 'Mink A' (Coopercraft). 3 GWR 4-plank open wagon (Coopercraft) and GWR 10-ton loco coal wagon (Coopercraft) (Ray Sinclair).

4, 5 *Modified Airfix kits.* **4** *GWR 24-ton 6-wheel 'Toad' brake van; 6-wheel milk tanker and GWR 20-ton loco coal wagon.* **5** *GWR Cordon (gas tank) wagon; APOC twin tank wagon; GWR ex-Barry Railway 20-ton 6-wheel brake van and GWR shunters truck (Ray Sinclair).*

Airfix underframes and repainted.

The accompanying photographs show some examples of the different kinds of construction described above. The unmodified Airfix range is not included as the prototypes are outside the period I model. I think they are well enough known not to need illustrating, and if you don't know what they're like, your local model shop is sure to have some. If you are modelling early BR, then the Airfix kits are good ones to start with. Modellers of the pre-Nationalisation scene will find a wide range of companies represented in the kit market—watch the model railway press or consult your dealer. With the vast range of kits now available you have no excuse for running inappropriate vehicles (unless you will insist on building the Listowel and Ballybunion in S gauge!), and your railway will be unique, because no one else will have exactly the same wagons as you have.

6 *Five private owner coal wagons constructed from Collett printed card body kits mounted on Peco underframes (Ray Sinclair).*

7 *Two wagons employing 'second-hand' Triang bodies; the tank wagon on a Peco underframe and the coal truck (fictitious owner!) on an Airfix mineral wagon chassis (Ray Sinclair).*

The gentle art of kit-bashing
or How to build a stone wagon from a tank car

Allan Dare

It's a fair guess that the most popular freight traffic on many model railways is quarry products—stone, sand and the like. The reasons are obvious. Quarries are often in scenic areas, and their rock faces and loading screens make attractive modelling subjects. The traffic is carried in a variety of interesting wagons, and the operating patterns often suit the small branch lines so many of us model. Finally, stone has been a staple traffic since the earliest days of the railways—and at no time more so than the present. The 'earth and stone' business has been one of British Rail's success stories in recent years, and heavy stone trains are to be seen all over the system.

Stone is carried in two types of wagons, which can be either owned by the railway, or by the quarry company. Where suitable unloading facilities exist, hopper wagons are preferred, and several fine models of these are now available. However, hoppers are not always suitable. Sometimes, the unloading facility consists of a 'tippler', which empties the wagon by bodily overturning it. In other instances the traffic may only be of short duration, in which case it is not worthwhile to install anything more sophisticated than a crane with a grab bucket. In these cases, a 'flat-bottomed' wagon is to be preferred. These are normally relatively simple vehicles, being little more than a box on wheels, without even any doors. They are very strongly constructed, so as to withstand the shock of having 20 or more tonnes of stone dropped into them when loading. Of course, in recent years they have been provided with modern brake gear and suspension, to allow for faster speeds and greater reliability. Whilst privately owned examples do exist, the majority of such wagons are BR owned, and are mostly used on traffic flows where it is not worth the customer's while to buy his own wagons.

In recent years, BR have used redundant Iron-Ore Tipplers (code MSO, MSV) for carrying stone; these wagons resemble the common 16.5 t mineral wagon, but without doors. However, the growth of traffic in the early 1970s meant that more wagons were needed. At the same

time, many fairly modern tank cars had been made redundant by the move to higher-capacity vehicles. The chassis of these tank cars were therefore combined with new bodywork to produce a long, low, four-wheel mineral wagon—the MTV. Photograph 1 shows some at Stoke-on-Trent, carrying glass-making sand. MTVs are used both by themselves and in company with older wagons, on a variety of flows. Typical are those of sand between Oakamoor and Wigan, and of stone from Penmaenmawr to Liverpool, and from the Mendips to Bletchley.

The MTV would seem a useful vehicle for any layout handling stone or sand traffic. Moreover, it is a very easy one to model. Not only is it simple in outline, but also the necessary chassis is available in the Airfix Esso tank wagon kit. If you have not built any wagons before, here is a good project to get started on! The materials you need are given in the accompanying table.

Parts list for MTV conversion

1 × Airfix 00-scale Esso tank wagon kit.
2 × 12 mm diameter 3-hole wheelsets, to suit.
4 × brass bearings, to suit.
2 × couplings, to suit.
30 thou Plastikard, or similar styrene sheet.
20 thou Plastikard, or similar styrene sheet.
Milliput epoxy filler, body putty, or similar.
SMS transfers, sheet A5, BR wagon code panels.
SMS transfers, sheet A6, live wire flashes.
Paint: BR bauxite brown, weathered, etc, black, white.

Start by cleaning away any flash on the Airfix chassis components. The solebars (parts 10 and 15) are then prepared by cutting away the small cylindrical projection about half way along, and then drilling out the holes in the axleboxes. This is done with a No 45 drill, to a depth of about 3 mm. Brass bearings can then be dropped into place, and secured with a drop of Plastic Weld. Which bearings you use will depend on your choice of wheels; the Peco cup style is for Peco and other plastic wheels, and the shouldered variety for use with pin-point axles. In the latter case, you will have to file smooth the back of the

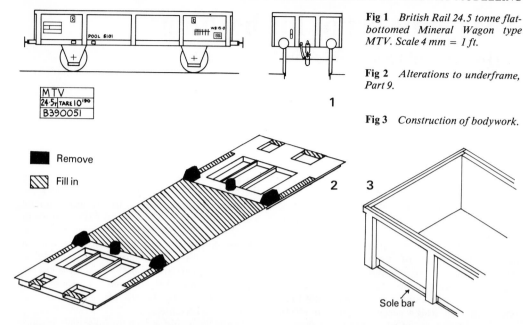

POOL 6101
W8 15-0

MTV
24·5ᴛ|TARE 10¹⁹⁰
B390051

Fig 1 *British Rail 24.5 tonne flat-bottomed Mineral Wagon type MTV. Scale 4 mm = 1 ft.*

Fig 2 *Alterations to underframe, Part 9.*

Fig 3 *Construction of bodywork.*

■ Remove

▨ Fill in

Sole bar

axleguard, in order to give sufficient clearance. (Of course, you can assemble the Airfix wheelsets, or even use other wheels in the original Airfix axlebox holes, but the improvement in running made by the use of proper bearings is well worth the extra effort). The next step is modify the underframe, (part 9) in accordance with Fig 2. Remove the tank cradles and locating spigots (shown in black on the drawing), and file smooth the surface of the end platforms. Then fill in the shaded areas with 0.20 styrene sheet; this ensures there are no unsightly gaps between the solebars and the floor which will be added. When all is dry, the solebars, wheelsets and underframe can be assembled as recommended by Airfix, followed by the remainder of the chassis components (parts 7-10, 15-21, 30-39). Omit the couplings and brake at this stage. Make sure that all is square, that the wheels run freely, and that brake shoes are not rubbing. You now have in effect a simple flat wagon, to which the body is to be added.

Building the body is simplicity itself. Start by cutting out the floor from 30 thou styrene, length 94 mm, width 30 mm. Sides, 94 mm by 14 mm, and ends, 32 mm by 14 mm, are cut from 20 thou sheet. These are cemented to the floor in the manner shown in Fig 3; the sides and ends fit outside the floor, and the ends overlap the sides. When dry, smooth down the joints if necessary with a file. The raves are cut from 30 thou sheet; 2 mm by 96 mm for the sides, 2 mm by 34 mm for the ends. Cement to the sides, so that the top

edges are flush, and the ends overlap the sides as in Fig 3. The body may now be assembled on to the chassis, making sure it is located square. The vertical strapping is made from 14 pieces of 30 thou styrene, 2 mm by 15 mm. Five are attached to each side, two on each end. Finally, use Milliput body putty, or similar, to fill in the gap between the vertical strapping and the solebar, as in Fig 3. Smooth off any joins in the bodywork, so that it better resembles all-welded construction.

Couplings are, of course, a matter of choice. If you are using Peco type, proceed as in the Airfix instructions. For Hornby, etc, 'tension lock' couplings, remove the spigots under the buffer beam, and glue on a packing piece 2 mm thick, to which the coupling can be attached. It is best to do this with a screw, as this gives extra strength. Three-link couplings will simply need a slot in the buffer beam. My favourite couplings are Kadee magnetics, and these are simply mounted by attaching the draftgear box to the underside of the chassis. Once you have added working couplings, the brake pipes (parts 28 and 29) and dummy couplings (parts 26 and 27) can be added according to the space available.

The entire wagon should now be painted in BR bauxite brown. Pick out the buffer heads, the axleguards and the brake gear in dirty black, and the end of the brake handle in white. The inside of the wagon is painted track colour, to reflect its rough service. Markings are as shown in Fig 1. All are in white, apart from the black

1 *Prototype MTVs at Stoke on Trent yard.*

2 *The model under construction, showing styrene sheet body before painting.*

3, 4 *The completed model.*

5 *The model on the author's layout.*

3

4

5

box in the right-hand corner of the body. If you model the Western Region, omit the pool number, and add a number in large figures above the left-hand box; 7641 would be typical. Don't forget the live wire warning flashes, the white triangle on the centre strap, the yellow load panel (which can be either on the body side or the solebar), and the label plate on the solebar. I used SMS transfers for lettering, adding detail with a 0.25 Rotring pen and UNO white ink.

Whilst the MTVs are basically BR wagons, similar vehicles run in private ownership. Amongst these are those used by Capper Pass Ltd to carry tin ore from Avonmouth to Birmingham. These are grey with red lettering. A photograph can be found in the Bradford

Barton book *B.R. Diesel Freight in the Era of Specialisation.*

Well, that's it. I hope that the MTV has proved an interesting, yet simple, project. It's a useful wagon in itself, and a good introduction to kit-bashing and scratch-building techniques. Plenty of scope exists for similar work; as an idea, and an ideal companion for the MTV, try building one of the older, short-wheelbase MSO or 'tipfit' wagons. You'll need the Airfix Mineral Wagon and Presflo kits—but I'll leave the rest up to you!

Likely locations for seeing MTVs: Oakamoor, Staffs; Stoke on Trent; Wigan (Co-op glass works); Bletchley; Redfern St, Sandhills (Liverpool); Penmaenmawr, North Wales—but don't trespass on railway or other property! ●

A track relaying unit

Ralph Fenwick

Some of the most interesting railway rolling stock and equipment is that designed for construction, maintenance and repair work on the line. Mostly they are seen on sidings at railway yards but, occasionally, particularly on a Sunday, we may catch a glimpse of them in action on the main line. Some of these units have been built or adapted in the railway workshops but many are the products of a number of specialist firms. Despite the intriguing appearance of these vehicles they have been generally neglected by the manufacturers of ready-to-run models and kits. Apart from a few railway cranes, very little is available for the enthusiast to run on his own layout.

My interest in such equipment was stimulated recently when I bought a copy of the book *BR Departmental Rolling Stock—A Pictorial Survey* by David Larkin and this model is based on the Track Relaying Unit (Southern Region TRU No 6) shown in the top photograph on page 45 of the book. The prototype is an LMS conversion of an ex-WD Warwell to a Bogie Bolster B from which the bolsters were later removed and a Coles crane mounted at either end. The cranes are self-powered so that a generator wagon is not required (an advantage over earlier TRUs) but the wagon is not self-propelled (as some later units are) needing a locomotive to move it. Two operators are required for the unit.

For ease of construction my model is not an exact replica of the prototype but it is based closely on it and does, I feel, give a reasonable representation of this unit. In fact, prototype special railway equipment is often not standard and many variations occur so the differences in the model are probably not significant! It is a relatively simple conversion project using the recently released and beautifully detailed Mainline Weltrol wagon, together with the Coles cranes from two Airfix RAF Recovery Set kits. It may seem rather extravagant to use two of these kits in this model but the cranes would be time consuming and difficult to scratch-build, whereas the conversion work is quick and easy and results in well-detailed crane units. It is also possible, of course, to use the left over parts from the kits to build motor vehicles or for detailing other models, and there are two beautifully detailed motor cycles included in each kit which can be utilised elsewhere on your layout.

I began construction with the two cranes, which are identical. There are basically two modifications which are required. The jibs are too long and must be shortened to allow the two cranes to be mounted at the ends of the wagon without the jibs fouling each other in the centre. The cranes would be too high if constructed as intended and they must be made lower; this is accomplished by mounting the jibs lower, so

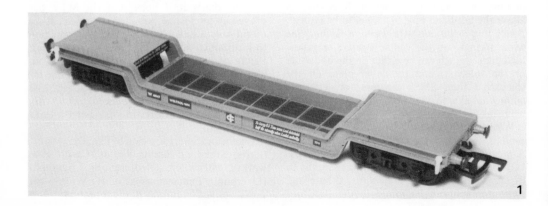

1

that they are closer to the crane bodies, and by reducing the thickness of the base mountings.

The jib sides (Parts 124 & 128—all Part numbers refer to the numbers used on the kit parts and on the kit instruction sheet) are shortened by cutting with a modelling knife or a razor saw to leave a section 73 mm long. The discarded pieces should have a 6 mm long section cut from the end of each. The top and bottom of each of these short pieces is filed down until the pieces will fit between the top and bottom girders of the 73 mm long jib sections, protruding slightly from the end. They are then cemented into place and will provide the holes into which the pulley will fit. The jib ends are then rounded off using a fine file. At this stage I painted the jib sides yellow using Humbrol MC2 Yellow Facings. Parts 127, 125 & 126 are then cemented onto Part 128 and a 25 cm length of black thread is placed over the two pulleys with equal lengths overhanging at each end. Hold the thread taut over the pulleys and fix in place by painting on solvent cement over each pulley. The two jib sides, Parts 124 & 128, are then glued together with Part 123 fitted between them, but not glued at present. The jib is then set aside while the crane body is assembled. Part 122 is reduced in thickness by approximately 2 mm by cutting away the rectangular part below the four protruding pieces with a razor saw. Part 137 is then fitted onto Part 122 and the part of the central rod which now extends below Part 122 is cut away. I decided for simplicity to fix the crane in the travelling position so I glued together Parts 122 and 137 at this stage. If you want your cranes to be able to rotate, leave these two parts separate. The middle section of Part 139 is cut down with the fine saw so that it is level with the upper margin of the sloping section of this piece. The crane body is then assembled by building up Parts 136, 138, 139,

140, 141, 142, 132, 133, 135 and 134 on to Part 137. There are two points to be noted here. One is that I fitted Parts 132, 133, 134 and 135 on to the body instead of the jib as shown in the kit instructions. This is because we will be mounting the jib lower than in the original model. The second point is that the small rectangular opening in Part 143 must be extended a little backwards because the rod of Part 134 will slope more due to the lower position of the jib. Part 143 is then fitted over the rod and cemented into place. I painted the crane body at this time, again using the Humbrol Yellow Facings. Once this was dry I positioned the jib between the supports (Parts 133 & 135) inserting the rod of Part 134 through the opening in Part 123. Note that the jib does not fit onto the small raised pivots as shown in the kit instructions but below this so that the top of the jib is horizontal and at a height of 10 mm above the top of the crane body. I fixed the jib in this position using solvent cement and also cemented the rod into Part 123. When firmly set I cut off the sections of Parts 133 & 135 which extended above the top of the jib using the razor saw. With a sharp modelling knife I trimmed off the excess rod flush with the top of Part 123. The visible sections of Parts 133 & 135 are then faced with thin plastic sheet cut to fit. This end of the black thread I passed down to Part 132 and fixed it in place by applying liquid cement with a brush.

Having assembled both cranes to this stage I set them aside, after completing the painting with Humbrol Yellow Facings, and turned my attention to the wagon. Relatively little modification is required. Strictly the sides and ends should be painted yellow though I haven't done so yet, mainly because it seems a shame to cover the excellent finish and lettering applied by the manufacturer! In fact the model looks quite attractive as it is, so I remain rather undecided

1 *The Mainline Weltrol wagon used for this conversion.*

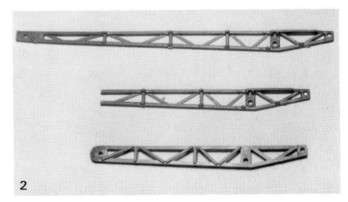

2 *The modifications to the crane jib sides are shown in this photograph. At the top is an unmodified jib side, while below this is a side which has been shortened to 73 mm. At the bottom is the completed side with the end added.*

2

about completing the painting. I fitted two lengths of Plastruct ⅛ in 'H' column (H-4) across the wagon near the centre with a gap of 8 mm between them. These provide fixing points for the crane hooks in the travelling position in which I have modelled the cranes. Between the girders there is space for two Merit tar barrels representing drums of fuel oil. I then cemented together Parts 129 and 130 of one hook and fixed the joined parts to the centre of one of the cross girders in the upright position, cementing the bottom of the hook on to the top of the girder. Once this was fixed firmly in place I took one of the assembled crane units and glued it onto the wagon at the corresponding end, positioning it so that the pulley at the end of the jib was directly above the hook on the girder. Again I waited until the glue had set firmly, then I looped the thread from the jib pulley around the hook pulley (Part 129) below and gently drew the thread taut. I applied solvent cement with a brush to the thread and pulley, holding the thread taut until it was fixed to the pulley. Then I took the free end up, threaded it through the jib and, again holding it taut, cemented it to the inner side of the pulley above. When the cement had set I trimmed off the excess thread with fine scissors. The addition of Part 131 then completed the hook assembly. The whole procedure was then repeated with the other crane.

The method I have described makes it fairly easy to keep the thread to the crane hooks taut, which is important for a realistic appearance, and this is an advantage of modelling the unit

fixed in the travelling/storage position. However, you may wish to make it possible for the crane units to be rotated so that the model can be placed in the working position. If so, do not cement Parts 122 and 137 together but leave them free so that Part 137, carrying the crane, can rotate on Part 122 which is fixed to the wagon. In this case you will not want to fix the hooks down to the girders but will need to leave them free. The hook assemblies are too light to hold the threads taut by their weight so you may like to try a trick I seem to recall reading about somewhere. This is to prepare the thread beforehand by rubbing white glue on to it then drawing it through your fingers to remove the excess. The thread is then hung up to dry with a weight on the end (a bulldog clip is convenient). You will find that the glue will give the thread more rigidity so that, though you can still curve it round the pulleys easily, it will tend to hang straight rather than with kinks and bends.

To complete the unit I fitted a 'Not to be loose shunted' sign on each side of the wagon as can be seen in the photograph of the finished model. These were reproduced photographically for me by a friend but we have provided a sign, printed to the correct size for the 00 gauge model, with this article for your convenience.

NOT TO BE LOOSE SHUNTED

Fig 1 *The sign for the wagon side is reproduced here the actual size for the 00-gauge model. It can be photocopied and mounted on thin card or plastic card for fixing on to the model.*

3   *The completed model track relaying unit.*

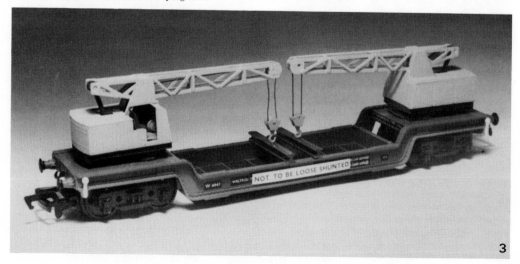

4 *A model of a small railway crane using the Airfix Coles crane. The prototype on which this model was based was used in a scrap yard in Newcastle.*

5 *Another conversion of the Airfix Coles crane is this mobile goods yard crane.*

Readers who refer to the prototype photograph in David Larkin's book will notice that there are diagonal black visibility stripes on the backs of the cranes. I didn't feel I could apply these neatly enough with paint but I hope eventually to use dry print black striping for this. There is also some lettering on the crane sides, 'TRU No 6' on the left hand unit (as we look at the wagon from the side) and 'Not to be loose shunted' on the right hand crane. This could also be applied with dry print lettering of appropriate size and could look every effective if done neatly. However, the model looks all right without this additional lettering and it is better to leave it off than to apply it imperfectly so I haven't yet decided whether to attempt adding it!

So there we have it. A fairly easy conversion which enables you to add a very unusual item of rolling stock to your layout. The Coles crane from the Airfix RAF Recovery Set kit is a very useful item for quite a variety of conversion projects of interest to the railway modeller. I have included pictures here of two such models built by Michael Andress. One is a light railway crane which was based on a prototype used in a scrap yard in Newcastle, and the other is a mobile crane suitable for a goods yard. To

6 *A British Rail light railway crane and match truck. The Airfix Coles crane body could be used for a model but the jib is of a different type and would need to be scratch-built.*

7   *A Hunslet mechanical trencher used for digging drainage trenches beside the line.*

8   *Plasser & Theurer produce a range of track maintenance equipment and this is one of their ballast tamping machines. It would be a scratch-builder's dream (or nightmare!) in model form.*

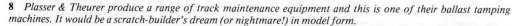

conclude there are also some photographs of other prototype non-revenue earning special railway vehicles which may be of interest and which, I hope, may appeal to some of you as possible modelling projects. The small crane could again utilise the Airfix Coles crane as a basis, but the rest of the equipment would have to be scratch-built models. The resulting models would certainly be unusual and eye-catching on your model railway layout.   ●

GWR goods depot—Somerset style

R. Petch

1

As a railway modeller with an interest mainly towards the scenic aspects, I was greatly excited at my first purchase of Peco Texture Modelling Compound. The thought of a railway scene dominated by solid stone structures, all in the same style, had great appeal and so I set to work with this new material. Disappointments usually follow fairly quickly after periods of great enthusiasm and my first attempt, a small stone cottage, was very much of an anti-climax. I found the walls tended to warp and I had difficulty in scribing the random stonework. I then invested in the booklet *Texture Modelling* by David Rowe and decided, for better or worse, to tackle something more ambitious.

I have always planned one day to have a fairly large layout of the GWR in Somerset and so, planning for the future, I looked around for suitable buildings to model in Texture Compound. R.H. Clark's *Historical Survey of Great Western Stations, Volumes One* and *Two* proved a great investment and my eyes eventually came to rest on Wookey Goods Depot (in the first volume). There is only one clear view of the depot taken from the road bridge looking north. This meant that the rear, with the loading bay and office, would need to be improvised.

To build a structure reasonably accurately from photographs, and without necessarily having any measurements, it is essential to draw it in the scale proportions required. I use large sheets of imperial graph paper which my local stationer sells in sets of three sheets 20 in × 30 in. The depot measurements are my own approximations and are shown on the plan. I also took the liberty of putting long skylights in the roof to give a little more light to the interior. The rear elevation shows my assumption that there would be two openings with sliding doors and steps leading up to the office door.

Now down to work. The first step is to cut sheets of 40 thou plastic card to the outline size, mark out all the windows, doors and entrances and cut these out with a craft knife and a straight-edge. The next stage is to cut lengths of $\frac{1}{2}$ in × $\frac{1}{8}$ in obeche strips to use as strengtheners behind the walls—a lesson I had learned after my first model. With the walls cut to shape and strengthened we are ready to apply the modelling compound.

Roll out a lump of texture compound on to a sheet of hardboard and flatten it with an old blunt knife or, if your daughter has a baking set, her mini rolling-pin will prove to be the best

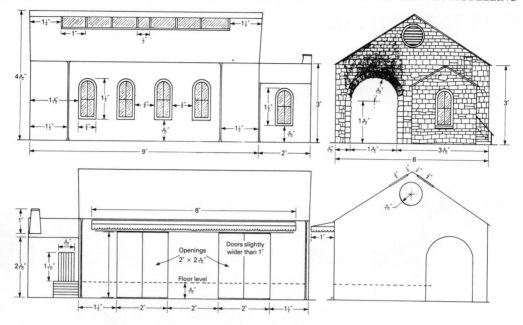

Plan of GWR goods depot.

implement. Roll out enough to do a small wall first and carefully peel it off the hardboard. Before laying it in place, cover the plastic card wall with PVA glue or another adhesive such as Evo-Stik. This will provide a bond between the compound and the smooth surface so that when the compound eventually dries out it will not fall away and should also be less inclined to crack.

With the compound laid out over the wall, carefully cut round the edges and openings with a sharp craft knife. After this stage it may be necessary to gently roll the surface again to ensure that the compound is evenly distributed before starting to scribe the stonework. If there are any rounded edges, such as the entrances and ventilators on both end walls, these should be scribed first, with the craft knife (and a steady hand!). Try not to score too deeply as this will weaken the contact with the plastic card. Next, score out the stonework with the aid of a steel straight-edge and space the rows of stone evenly, which will give a regular stone block effect. If the wall is laid on graph paper whilst scribing, the spacing of each row can easily be marked off. One must remember to keep the vertical joints in a straight line and not to extend them beyond the horizontal lines. It is essential to keep the knife blade perfectly clean while this operation is in progress so as to achieve an even depth of cut. If a mistake is made then smooth

out the area and start again—what could be simpler!

With the first wall complete, one can sit back and admire the work. From now on each wall becomes a little easier and, hopefully, a little more satisfying. It is worth mentioning here that some modellers prefer to glue the walls together and complete the shell before embarking on the texture compound technique but I prefer to work on the walls individually. When scribing around windows and doors etc, I found it necessary to trim the compound again as it may expand slightly after laying a straight-edge on it.

After a few hours the compound begins to harden and that is when the warping can occur. To overcome this, lay each wall between two books making sure that the texture is hard enough to hold its shape. Once again, two volumes of R.H. Clark's *Great Western Stations* come in handy! Slight warping may still occur and this is due to the size of wallspace—the smaller the section, the less this will happen. After a day or two, the compound should be thoroughly dry and the walls can be held up together to get the first real idea of what the finished article will look like. I prefer to paint the walls before glueing together. Each wall is laid out and a coat of light grey (Humbrol 64) applied. A very pleasing finish is obtained by

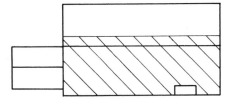

Fig 1

picking out stones in different shades of grey and adding a liberal shade of black with a dry brush to the portals and tops of the ventilators.

The window frames are cut out from thin card and the office door from scribed plastic card. (I shall leave the rear access doors until later.) The windows and door are then painted in GW cream and later glazed and glued in place, together with the office door. The walls can now be glued together, starting with the office, which can be set aside to dry while the main structure is glued together. The walls are then stood on a flat surface to ensure a true vertical joint. I used Evo-Stik for all gluing operations as it provides a good bond on impact. If the walls do not butt perfectly then Polyfilla can be used to cover any joints, followed by a little touching up with paint.

I next considered the floor. I originally cut out and scribed a piece of thick card $3\frac{1}{2}$ in $\times$ $8\frac{3}{4}$ in and trimmed it to fit across two obeche strips, one glued inside the bottom rear wall and the other between the entrances $\frac{1}{4}$ in from the foot of the portals. I then decided, as in Fig 1, to have one loading bay slightly recessed which involved cutting out a piece of floor and removing the bottom section of the wall and setting it back by just over an inch. This will allow vehicles to back into the depot to load/unload. Before glueing in place, the floor is painted in a light brown shade. I then cut four lengths of $\frac{1}{4}$ in square obeche to go across the top of the walls as support beams but eight would probably have looked better. These are glued in place ensuring the ends would not interfere with the slope of the roof.

The roofing technique is simple and effective. I cut out a large piece of thick card sufficient to overlap by about $\frac{1}{8}$ in at each end. I then scored the centre line, folded it and let it rest on the gables to ensure the correct fit was achieved and any trimming done accordingly. The window area is cut out and the card roof glued to the gables. Next, a sheet of very fine wet and dry paper (dark grey) is marked out in $\frac{1}{4}$ in squares and cut into strips. The $\frac{1}{4}$ in marks along each

strip are clipped with scissors making sure not to snip right through too often! The result is a row of slates which can be glued to the card roof and each successive layer overlapped and aligned for the correct spacing. The ends are then trimmed and the window area glazed. I used plastic micro strip to strengthen the glazed area and a strip of card across the top to form the ridge tiles. Plastic strips and rodding are then painted cream and glued in position as barge boards, guttering and downpipes respectively.

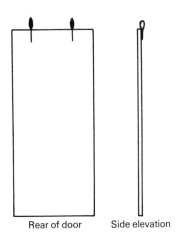

Rear of door   Side elevation

Fig 2

The sliding doors are made from plastic card and scribed to give the effect of planking with lengths of micro strip at the top, bottom and a diagonal added. Now for a little added ingenuity. The doors can be made to slide by using split pins. A length of piano wire is cut about 8 in long and bent at $\frac{1}{4}$ in from the ends. Two holes are then drilled into the wall ready to take the wire which will act as a rail for the sliding doors. If all four doors are to open, slide eight split pins on to the wire and then glue these pins to the top and back of the doors, as shown in Fig 2. When dry, pick up the rail and attached doors and glue the ends of the rail into the holes. It is probably best to have a dry run first in case

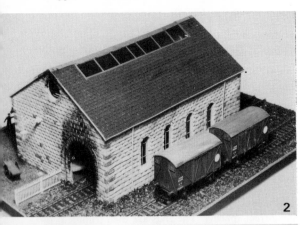

2

3

4

5

the doors do not have the required clearance and the holes need to be re-drilled. Your depot can now accommodate the bustle of activity on market day or shut down for Sunday.

The canopy is made from plastic card, scribed for planking effect and surrounded by Slaters canopy valance—another very useful product. All that remains is to add those little touches of realism, such as the Mikes Models Lamps, the horse and cart and the foreman turning up on his motorbike. The odd wall notice and the 'Goods Office' complete the scene.

The depot is now ready to take its place on the layout. The objective has been to build a stone structure, typical of those seen over most of the Great Western network—something to give the layout real atmosphere, without necessarily being exact down to the last stony detail. Just as a point of interest, I recently went to Somerset for a day out and found myself at Wookey. Imagine my amazement on finding Wookey Depot still standing and very much in action, now used as a forge. The first surprise was that the stonework is not grey but red—black and white photos never tell the truth! The second surprise came when I walked around the back to find only a single loading bay but with a large round arch entrance—quite artistic really. Ah well, you can't win them all—it's back to the drawing board, lads!   ●

1, 2, 3, 4, 5 *Five views of the completed model.*

Where there's a wall there's a way!

Allan Downes

A model building, whether it is put together with machined perfection or just held together with Sellotape, is only as good as its final outward appearance, which relies mainly on the wall and roof finish. Often one sees a building during the course of construction where the interior former work is an art in itself, quite without necessity and a shame to be hidden forever beneath the roof!

There are three basic materials used throughout model building construction, namely cardboard, styrene sheet and balsa wood. Whilst styrene and balsa have their certain disadvantages, cardboard does not seem to have any. I may appear to sound a little biased here in my way of thinking since I use nothing else but card for my own purposes, but this was not until after having done battle with other materials. First I find that only a solvent glue will hold plastic together and wood glue is required for balsa, whereas anything (even jam!) will stick cardboard. Also one has to consider the reactions of these materials when subjected to deep cuts with a modelling knife where, for example, cutting numerous door and window openings out of 40 thou thick styrene sheet isn't exactly fun with the knife blade only too ready to go careering across the surface in the general direction of your fingers. Balsa wood reacts in much the same fashion by insisting that it should be cut along its own natural grain in preference to your marked line!

However, the choice of modelling materials is a personal one. As all my own work is based on card the following wall texture methods may not work on other materials but, since card is extremely versatile, cuts cleanly and costs little, why not give it a try. The type of wall finishes one would expect to come up against are actually very few, being mainly housebrick, random stone, dressed stone, flint, rubble and washed plaster, all of which can be convincingly reproduced in scenic modelling without too much effort. Because the wall finish and texture on a building provides its final and finished image on the human eye then it must warrant a little effort on the modeller's part.

Dealing with the common housebrick first and trying to forget about embossed and printed brickpaper sheets, I will describe, for what it is worth, my own method where computer punchings are used. Though these small 'chads' are only suitable in 4 mm scale the same method can still be applied for other scales where, of course, the modeller will have to cut the bricks in batch form from postcards, which does not really seem a good idea at all, though this is what I had to do in the past before I discovered that multi-million dollar computers have at least one good function!

Bricklaying method

Mark the four main walls of the building out onto a sheet of non-faced card 1 mm thick then cut out, also cut out all window and door apertures. Rule horizontal lines 5 mm apart across each wall section where this spacing will accommodate three rows of bricks and mortar joints exactly. Work with each wall section separately flat down on the table and start by spreading a thin layer of Evo-Stik woodworking glue along the first margin. Here the computer punchings are picked up by prodding with a knife point and are laid directly onto the glue which will hold the bricks firmly enough for the knife to be released. Work the first course along the entire length of the wall section, then lay the third course tight along the 5 mm margin line exactly opposite the first row. The second row can now be laid in between the first and third but, of course, offset to give the brick bonding.

By working the courses in this manner all bricks will run straight without the risk of running out of true, as might easily happen if attempted without the 5 mm guide lines. At first progress will appear to be painfully slow but familiarity will breed speed and you will be surprised how fast you can cover a wall section with individual bricks. From experience I have found that an average sized building can be bricked out in two evenings or in one day if you are prepared to sit there and stay with it!

The reward, of course, is the final outcome. Printed and embossed sheets cannot hope to

1   *Thatched cottages are all 'round and plump' and appear as if they have just grown out of the ground. This model scene took around four weeks to create, using the methods referred to in the text.*

2   *Another view of the village scene where the effect of the stone wall press can be judged. The thatching is imitated by strands of wool glued across the roofs, flocked with brown flock powder and then dyed.*

match the effect and realism for such sheets are machine produced and much too accurate to give any true effect of brick work which, in real life, is man's strained effort in trying to achieve a straight line with warped blocks of clay floating about on a bed of mortar! Computer punchings can never be laid really perfectly straight which, in the end, turns out to be an advantage; your wall will start to match the prototype where imperfect rows give the unmistakable character of the common house-brick.

Where it comes to window apertures and wall ends, simply lay the bricks running proud over the edges where the bonding dictates and trim back clean afterwards when all has dried out. The final colouring and toning of the brickwork is most important and, what I have found to be most effective, takes only a few minutes to apply. First brush light strokes of well thinned Evo-Stik woodworking glue across the entire bricked surface in a 'hit and miss' fashion and then leave for ten minutes to dry. When the wall section has dried, apply a single coat of Colron

Peruvian Mahogany Wood Dye—available from most Do It Yourself shops—then sit back and watch the results. The varied tones seen in real brickwork will materialise in seconds as the areas of brickwork that took the thinned glue will weaken the penetration of the dye and the areas that were missed out will show fuller and darker tones. Drying time with the wood dye is around one hour, after which the door and window detail can be added and then the completed sections are assembled as you would assemble a model kit. The roof can now be cut and laid flat down on the table ready for tiling. The method I used for this is as follows:

Batch six postcards together and mark out 4 mm squares on to the top card. Using a sharp knife cut first along the horizontal lines and then down the vertical lines to produce hundreds of small tiles in only a few minutes. To hold the six cards rigid whilst cutting it is best to rig up some kind of cutting block out of chipboard. This will make life a lot easier when trying to produce perfectly square tiles in such quantity. Laying is much the same as for the brickwork but, of course, each row has to overlap the one below by about half. Work in stints again and you will find that a few hours work will be rewarded by a very realistic roof finish. Colouring is with Colron Peruvian Mahogany Wood Dye again, brushed straight on to the card tiles. No pre-wash of thinned glue is required.

Stonework

The method described here was used to produce the stonework seen on the buildings in the accompanying photographs and once you are geared for this method it is extremely quick and effective. First one needs a stonewall press. Begin by rolling out a $\frac{1}{2}$-in slab of Plasticine 4 in long by 2 in wide. With an electrician's screwdriver, fashion a stonewall effect into the Plasticine. Take a lot of care and effort with this because the entire success of your press relies on this Plasticine mould; make sure each stone is cut deep into the Plasticine and has a good clean definition. Once you are satisfied with this, build up a Plasticine wall about $\frac{3}{4}$ in high around the mould, making sure that it is watertight. Next a tin of clear casting resin is required—good handicraft shops stock this—to be mixed up to the appropriate quantity. Simply pour this into the mould from one end; this way the liquid will flow forward, forcing the air out before it. The filled mould should now be left on a dead flat surface for 24 hours before removing it. If, after this period, the resin has set hard, peel away the Plasticine, scrubbing the surplus away from the

stonework side of the casting. You will now have a press that will enable you to produce random stonewalling in only seconds and literally save you hundreds of hours of work.

To produce a stone cottage, try this method. Cut the walls out of 1 mm thick card, as per bricked buildings, spread a thin layer of Evo-Stik woodworking glue over the entire wall section and spread a 3-4 mm thick layer of Pyruma (or Kos) Fire Cement over the glue. With the compound evenly spread, sprinkle on a dusting of talcum powder to act as a releasing agent and then simply apply the press with reasonable pressure and then release. The effect is instantaneous and the press is now used again and again until the whole wall is covered. Continued and offset pressing will chop the stonework up even smaller and, if the press is applied about six times or so, you will invariably end up with a very realistic flint or rubble stone wall finish.

Any compound that squeezes out across window apertures and over wall ends can be trimmed back flush with the modelling knife. Pyruma Fire Cement is a plastic based compound used for repairing cracked fireplaces and therefore only sets rock hard under such extreme heat conditions; if left to dry naturally it will eventually harden out but will be seen to crumble after a period of time, particularly if subjected to damp. Therefore, to safeguard against this, I bake each prepared wall section for about ten minutes in a medium oven. I might add that the whole baking process takes around 60 minutes, 50 of which are taken up trying to convince the wife that ovens have other uses than for burning pies in! The wall sections, when dried, will tend to warp considerably but slight pressure will flatten them; you will hear audible cracking noises as you do this due to the rock hard compound cracking but since the cracks will follow the line of least resistance they will go unnoticed inside the stonework joins. Colouring can be applied using dyes, poster, water or even oil-based paints and indeed a wash of well thinned matt black will result in a very convincing worn stone texture.

Chimneys can be built up by coating a length of batten with Pyruma, then working the press into the compound and baking in the oven. Once hardened this 'chimney stick' can be sawn into lengths as required and set down into the roof. Other equally good effects can be obtained by pressing a section of crêpe-soled shoe into soft Pyruma, stippling with a nail brush and even pressing coarse sandpaper into compound. Beneath the soles of the shoes we wear are many interesting 4 mm possibilities and often we are walking on the answer to the problem at hand!

Many everyday materials can be put to good use in the world of scenic modelling where, for instance, a natural concrete finish can be obtained by dusting actual neat cement powder over glue, rubbing over lightly when dry and then sealing with hair lacquer. Stucco effects are possible by using Artex powder over glue and then painting with thinned emulsion. Diamond sand over glue will produce ideal road surfaces and stoneshot walling. Budgie grit glued to a card building shell is an almost perfect replica in miniature of flint and even talcum powder over glue will work wonders for white rendered cottages or town buildings.

The scenic modeller then should never really be stuck for an answer and, if in doubt, take a stroll into the larder or root around in the garden shed. Such places provide the essence that model railways are made of—try dried sago, for instance, embedded in Pyruma for cobblestones, and I have a distinct feeling that somewhere there is a more positive use for cornflakes and, without doubt, the cake icing set . . . .   ●

3 *A detailed shot of a stucco finish town building. The windows are an extremely important feature and much care should be taken over their construction. Often ornate bay windows can transform a plain mundane building into one of character and interest.*

4 *Corner buildings should always 'come round easy' as opposed to having sudden right angles. This will permit both an attraction to the eye and room for some interesting feature work.*

Buildings for Hampton South

Pat Saunders

Hampton South is the terminus station of an 00-gauge layout which has been built by myself and two friends, Peter Smith and David Heulin. The layout represents a section of the old Southern Railway in the period between the two world wars and, while the station is not based on any one prototype, it is typical of the area being modelled. In contrast to the more usual country branch line in its rural landscape, an urban setting was chosen as it was felt that this would give interest and atmosphere in the limited space available.

The layout had to be portable and the baseboard was therefore designed to hinge at the centre. When folded up the total depth of the baseboard is only 9 inches so that the height of any structures to be fitted on to the layout would be quite restricted. To allow the maximum possible height for the buildings they were placed so that those on one section of the baseboard would interlock with those on the other when the baseboard was folded up. This imposed some restrictions on the positioning of the structures and other fittings on the layout. We also wanted the railway to have reasonable operating potential with the result that the track itself occupied much of the baseboard area, leaving relatively little space for structures and scenery. Careful planning was therefore required in the selection, size and location of the buildings so that those which could be accommodated would be as effective as possible in creating the appearance and atmosphere of the rather grimy and neglected areas so often found adjacent to the railway tracks in towns and cities.

Once we knew the sites available on the layout for structures and had decided on the effect we wanted how could we achieve this most easily and successfully? There are many excellent buildings, mostly in the form of card or plastic kits, available from model railway shops and we first considered these. Despite their good features there are disadvantages in using these models. One is that the buildings often appear on model railway layouts, making them familiar to the viewer and reducing their effectiveness in creating a realistic scene. Because of this some skill is required in placing and grouping them convincingly. There may also be the problem of a kit structure not fitting the site exactly and requiring adaptation. Often the architectural style is unsuitable for the area or district you are modelling. For these reasons we decided that we would build our own structures from scratch. Though this may sound more difficult initially it can often be more convenient in the end than trying to modify kit models to make them suitable for your own particular needs. It is also more satisfying and certainly cheaper!

Scratch-built structures can be constructed to fit the sites available exactly and can also be selected to give just the effect wanted. For example, with the appropriate choice of proportions and architectural style a single row of buildings can suggest a crowded, built-up area. With the detailed brick papers and the brick-finish embossed plastic sheet materials that are readily available from model shops, a good finished appearance is easy to achieve. The modeller can choose to copy an actual prototype building exactly down to the last detail, or can merely use the basic features of a structure as a guide. Much depends on personal preference and on the skill of the modeller and on the time that can be spent on construction. In our case time was a major consideration and the buildings shown in the accompanying photographs were all produced quite quickly at a very modest outlay. None of the structures are exact models of actual buildings but all are based on close observation of the real thing.

In making the buildings for Hampton South, various construction methods have been tried but most of the models are finished with brick-embossed plastic sheet material. In fact, since discovering this useful material I have not used the more conventional colour printed brick papers at all. The embossed plastic needs backing so a basic structure of either stout card or thicker plain plastic sheet was built for each model. Regarding the choice of card or plastic there are pros and cons for each but I do find the card buildings easier to work on generally.

1 *Hampton South station building. Note the many small details on the platforms, adding to the interest of the scene.*

2 *The signal cabin at Hampton South.*

3 *The goods shed in the foreground and the water tank at the rear of the layout conceal the hinges joining the two sections of this portable layout.*

4, 5 *The interesting selection of typical small industrial and commercial buildings has created a very realistic effect. Most of these structures are modelled in low relief and occupy very little space.*

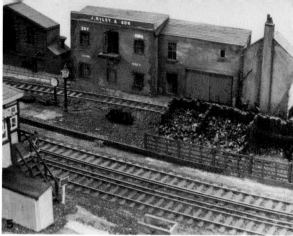

Various types of card have been used. The most frequently employed is what I personally refer to as a 'strawboard', a sort of coarse-grained card used as backing on pads of tear-off forms used at my work. Other card used has included ordinary corrugated card boxes cut into sheets; if uncreased this card is very strong, though light, and makes an ideal backing material.

For the buildings made entirely from plastic (the row of shops, the signal box, and the station) my construction technique is now fairly standardised. I start with the brick-embossed plastic card. As the edge of the sheet is often not parallel to the brick courses, check this and, if it is not, trim the lower edge of the sheet along a mortar line using a sharp modelling knife guided by a straight-edge or steel ruler. As none of my buildings are exact scale models I save time and make life easier by marking out the walls of a building directly on to the plastic, using the brick courses as a guide. Following a rough sketch made on scrap paper I draw the walls out on the plastic, keeping things even by counting the courses or following a line with a straight-edge. The doors and windows are shaded in and very quickly the basic appearance of the building becomes apparent. At this stage I can make any adjustments or alterations that I feel are necessary. When marking out it is important to make allowance for any extension of the building walls below the scenery ground level. Some modellers like to construct their buildings in this way so that, when the scenery is modelled, it can be brought up to ground level and there will be no risk of having any unsightly and unrealistic gaps between the building bases and the ground. It may also be necessary to construct buildings in this way if the ground surface is to slope between the front and rear of a building. I usually leave some depth when marking out, just in case I need it. If not, it can easily be removed just prior to assembling the walls.

Having marked out the walls to my satisfaction, I cut them out using a sharp modelling knife with a steel rule or straight-edge. I then add any extra brick facings which are required. Often it will be found that the area at damp course level is reinforced by additional layers of bricks, especially on older or industrial buildings. Window sills can be represented by strips of brick cut across the courses. Sometimes further additional brick layers are present just below the roof line. By applying strips of brick cut from embossed plastic card where they look right, a convincing relief effect can be built up. The strips are best attached by means of one of the solvent cements (available under various trade names) applied with a brush. The liquid bonds the plastic immediately and without the slightest mess. The only need for caution is that repeated applications to the same area can soften the whole depth of the plastic and, if this is occurring, the wall is best left for 24 hours to harden again.

The brick-embossed plastic sheet on its own is much too flimsy for walls and it must be attached to a backing of card or plastic card. The cut out brick wall is laid on plain plastic sheet of suitable thickness or on stout card. Windows, doors and any other openings are marked out by running a pencil around the inside of the apertures. The brick wall is now set aside while the openings are removed from the backing. For the windows the cuts are made further out than the guide lines to take the clear plastic used for glazing. Window framing can be made from thin plastic strip and fitted into place after the basic glazing is carried out. In the case of the shop fronts where large areas of window glass are present, the plastic glazing itself acts as the backing with extra support added where found necessary.

The walls are then assembled to form a box-like structure. For appearances the larger face is

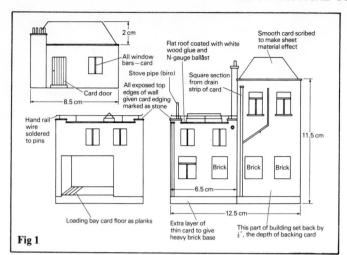

Fig 1 *See photograph 4.*

Fig 1

- 2 cm
- All window bars — card
- Stove pipe (biro)
- Flat roof coated with white wood glue and N-gauge ballast
- Smooth card scribed to make sheet material effect
- Square section from drain strip of card
- All exposed top edges of wall given card edging marked as stone
- Card door
- 8.5 cm
- Hand rail wire soldered to pins
- 11.5 cm
- Brick   Brick   Brick
- 6.5 cm
- 12.5 cm
- Loading bay card floor as planks
- Extra layer of thin card to give heavy brick base
- This part of building set back by ⅛", the depth of backing card

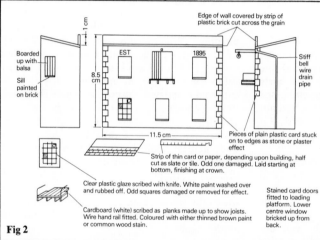

Fig 2 *See photograph 5.*

Fig 2

- Edge of wall covered by strip of plastic brick cut across the grain
- 1 cm
- Boarded up with balsa
- Sill painted on brick
- EST   1895
- 8.5 cm
- 11.5 cm
- Stiff bell wire drain pipe
- Pieces of plain plastic card stuck on to edges as stone or plaster effect
- Strip of thin card or paper, depending upon building, half cut as slate or tile. Odd one damaged. Laid starting at bottom, finishing at crown.
- Clear plastic glaze scribed with knife. White paint washed over and rubbed off. Odd squares damaged or removed for effect.
- Cardboard (white) scribed as planks made up to show joists. Wire hand rail fitted. Coloured with either thinned brown paint or common wood stain.
- Stained card doors fitted to loading platform. Lower centre window bricked up from back.

Fig 3 *See photograph 5.*

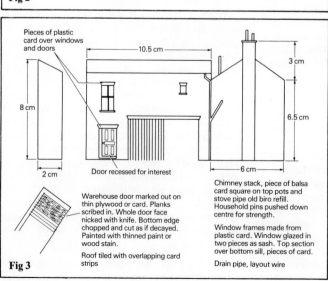

Fig 3

- Pieces of plastic card over windows and doors
- 10.5 cm
- 3 cm
- 8 cm
- 6.5 cm
- 2 cm
- Door recessed for interest
- 6 cm
- Warehouse door marked out on thin plywood or card. Planks scribed in. Whole door face nicked with knife. Bottom edge chopped and cut as if decayed. Painted with thinned paint or wood stain.
- Roof tiled with overlapping card strips
- Chimney stack, piece of balsa card square on top pots and stove pipe old biro refill. Household pins pushed down centre for strength.
- Window frames made from plastic card. Window glazed in two pieces as sash. Top section over bottom sill, pieces of card.
- Drain pipe, layout wire

Fig 4 *Lean-to—see photograph below. The wooden bracing at the side of this building is a typical but seldom modelled feature.*

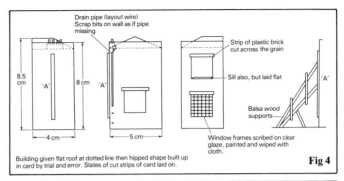

Drain pipe (layout wire)
Scrap bits on wall as if pipe missing

Strip of plastic brick cut across the grain

Sill also, but laid flat

8.5 cm   'A'   8 cm   'A'

'A'

Balsa wood supports

4 cm   5 cm

Window frames scribed on clear glaze, painted and wiped with cloth.

Building given flat roof at dotted line then hipped shape built up in card by trial and error. Slates of cut strips of card laid on.

Fig 4

Fig 5 *See photograph 5.*

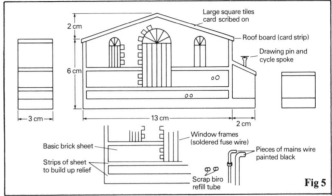

Large square tiles card scribed on

2 cm

Roof board (card strip)

Drawing pin and cycle spoke

6 cm

3 cm   13 cm   2 cm

Window frames (soldered fuse wire)

Basic brick sheet

Pieces of mains wire painted black

Strips of sheet to build up relief

Scrap biro refill tube

Fig 5

Fig 6 *Terrace of houses. See photograph 7.*

Fig 7 *Terrace of shops. See photographs 6 and 7.*

Roof detail as shops, depth 2 cm. Terrace cut from single sheet of embossed plastic card. Windows glazed from rear, curtains painted various greys or buff tissue. Sills/frames/lintels added from strip plastic card, painted matt colours. All plastic construction, assembled completely with solvent cement.

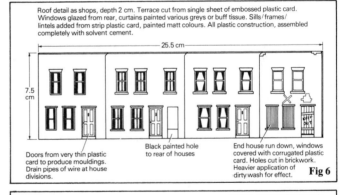

25.5 cm

7.5 cm

Doors from very thin plastic card to produce mouldings. Drain pipes of wire at house divisions.

Black painted hole to rear of houses

End house run down, windows covered with corrugated plastic card. Holes cut in brickwork. Heavier application of dirty wash for effect.

Fig 6

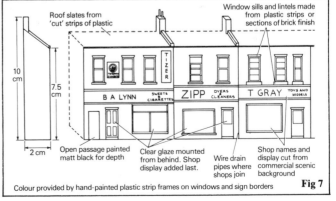

Roof slates from 'cut' strips of plastic

Window sills and lintels made from plastic strips or sections of brick finish

10 cm

7.5 cm

TIZER

B A LYNN   SWEETS CIGARETTES   ZIPP   DYERS CLEANERS   T GRAY   TOYS AND MODELS

2 cm   Open passage painted matt black for depth

Clear glaze mounted from behind. Shop display added last.

Wire drain pipes where shops join

Shop names and display cut from commercial scenic background

Colour provided by hand-painted plastic strip frames on windows and sign borders

Fig 7

6

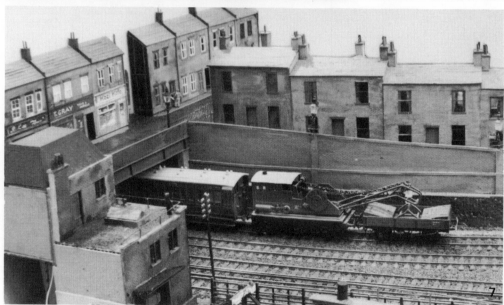

7

6, 7 Terraced houses and shops have been modelled and positioned to give an accurate representation of the rather run down urban areas often seen adjacent to the railway tracks in towns and cities.

best made to overlap the smaller when joining corners. Even better is to mitre the corners but this is rather time consuming. With card backing it is usually possible to separate the walls again if a mistake is made in assembly but with plastic the walls, once stuck together, are difficult to

get apart so there is less chance of making any adjustment later. The basic box made up from the sides is then strengthened by the addition of internal floors or bracing. Warping can be a problem if different materials are combined, for example, brick-embossed plastic sheet and card backing. I have found, however, that any tendency to warp is very much reduced by attaching scraps of plastic to the inside surface of the card or by adding as much bracing as possible. On larger buildings I have used the corrugated card and this seems unaffected, needing only minimal bracing and no plastic reinforcement. Tweezers are useful for fitting bracing as fingers often seem too large and also tend to get smeared with solvent. The latter is most undesirable as there is the risk of producing fingermarks on the plastic surface and these cannot be removed without damage to the brick surface.

It is worth while checking at various stages from now onwards what will be visible of the interior of the building. If nothing can be seen then it is hardly worth the effort of adding complete interior details. If there are large openings in the walls and the interior is clearly visible then the interior should be detailed to avoid an empty, unrealistic appearance. In most cases just a suggestion of fixtures inside, for example, a table near a window, dimly visible through tissue paper curtains will be perfectly adequate. Visible white interior surfaces are best painted over in a dark colour.

Doors can be made up in plastic or card, including the frame. On all the buildings there is a flat sub-roof with the hipped shapes added afterwards. Again the shape is made up largely by eye. The roofing is plain material, card or plastic, with the tiles being added last, after the chimneys. These can be made from wood strip, plastic or pieces of dowel. I have found that they are best fitted so that they extend through the hipped roof to be supported by the flat sub-roof inside. Any unsightly gaps around the chimneys soon disappear when the stack is faced with brick and the tiles are laid up to it. The tiles are lengths of paper or thin card or plastic card depending on what the roof is made of and on the amount of relief required. The strips are cut half way across at intervals and are laid on the roof in overlapping rows, giving the effect of individual tiles. Odd tiles are partly cut away to make them look as if they are damaged. Real chimney pots vary considerably in shape and various items can be used to model them. On the station the chimney pots are butchered milk churns while on other buildings they are pieces of used biro tube or plastic rod. The peculiar stack on the lean-to is part of a cycle spoke and a drawing pin. Drain pipes can be made from odd bits and pieces to be found around the home. The plastic covered solid core type of electrical wire used for layouts is useful for round pipes, while strips of card or plastic can represent square section pipes. Many other small details can be added from scraps of wood, card or plastic using real buildings as a guide.

Brick paper is available in a range of different colours and types and, if you use this on your models, all that is usually required for a realistic finish is some weathering to give the effect of dirt and grime. The brick embossed plastic sheet is produced in white, red or buff. I always use the red as this gives a good red brick finish with a minimum of effort. Once the building is assembled all that is needed is a dirty wash of diluted matt black paint, the surplus being mopped up with a cloth. This wash runs into nooks and crannies giving a dingy neglected look to the structure. Any paint used for doors, window frames, and so on should always be matt. I never use gloss paint on any buildings. The most useful colours are the various shades of matt greys and browns. The only bright colours one might expect to see near a steam railway yard are window displays in the shops. Small pieces of tissue, tiny scraps of card and blobs of colour can be used to suggest the contents of the shop windows but this can be rather fiddly. A fairly easy and effective method is to buy a commercial printed colour scenic background which includes shop fronts, then cut these out and build them into the shops. This was the method used for the low relief shops at Hampton South. Plastic lettering, available from model shops in a variety of sizes, can be used to produce very neat names for shops and other buildings. These can be attached to the brick plastic sheet with a dab of solvent cement and painted when dry.

There are many other small details which can be added using real buildings as your guide; slight variations in brick colours, cracks in walls, brackets, lamps, broken windows, signs, and so on. The buildings you produce will give your layout its individual character. Construction is a lot easier than it sounds and confidence will come with experience. Start by looking at the real thing; take a walk around the area near your local station and make a few sketches of buildings and details that interest you. Then try converting these into models for your layout.

All the buildings and features seen in the photographs were produced by the joint efforts of Peter Smith, David Huelin and myself. The success of our first 'townscape' has led to the planning of another baseboard, extending further into the town, and to a search for suitable structures for it. ●

A cottage scene in 4 mm scale

R. Petch

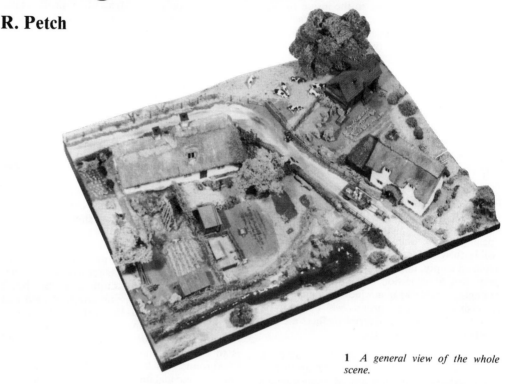

1 *A general view of the whole scene.*

The most embracing aspect of the model railway hobby must be the unlimited scope available to the enthusiast who wishes to fully exploit his talents. The extent to which one can delve into scratch-building locos and rolling stock, into electronic circuitry and the finest detail of modelling scenery and buildings usually ends up with each of us tending to specialise in one particular field. The great advantage of the local club or society is that these individual skills are pooled, often resulting in complete layouts of very high standard being put together and exhibited. It is from such exhibitions that enthusiasm and inspiration surges and new blood is drawn into the hobby.

Another venue where such enthusiasm and dedication abounds is the Pendon Museum near Abingdon. It was while studying their quaint cottages and country scenes that I was inspired to build a modest scene of my own design—small but packed with detail, something to decorate a corner of the lounge and to interest young and old alike. Why not? After all, people admire oil paintings, ornate pieces of furniture or illuminated tropical fish tanks.

I made a rough sketch of the scene in which I

wanted to include a country lane, a couple of cottages, some outbuildings, well cultivated cabbage patches and a stream or pond. I did not contemplate modelling individual flowers or leaves on trees as this level of detail was not absolutely essential to my objective and would be very time consuming. However, while still at the planning stage, Hammant and Morgan conveniently put their Woodland Scenic materials on the market.

The overall model measures 52 cm × 70 cm (20$\frac{1}{2}$ in × 27$\frac{1}{2}$ in) and took about 40 hours to complete over a period of six weeks. I started with a $\frac{1}{2}$ in chipboard base on to which I screwed four pieces of 1 in × 1 in batten along the sides and flush with the base. I then made a rough contoured drawing the same size as the base on which I showed the positions of the cottages, stream and lane. From this the slope of the land could be judged and the hardboard facia cut to shape accordingly. The highest and lowest points on the facia measure 8 cm and 4 cm. The sides were then nailed to the battens with panel pins.

I then followed a similar method of landscape modelling to that adopted by the Pendon boys. Lengths of thick card were cut in 52 cm lengths and contoured to match the left-hand facia. Each successive strip was contoured and glued in position with 20 mm spacers and the final strip was then matched with the right-hand facia contour and glued in place. Having planned where the buildings would go, and their overall dimensions, I cut the card strips to form a well in which each cottage would sit.

For the next stage I obtained a length of cotton scrim from a local car accessory shop and cut out a piece which would stretch across the whole baseboard. It may be necessary to use more than one piece depending on the size of the material. The scrim is then glued to the top edges of the hardboard and card strips. When secure, trim the edges and around the holes where the buildings will fit. This tough base is then covered by an earth mix of Polyfilla and fine sawdust to which is added helpings of Burnt Sienna and Black Rowney powder paints. This provides an excellent earthy finish and if laid on reasonably thickly, should take a few days to dry thoroughly. This is quite an exciting stage as one gains the first real perspective of what the scene will be like.

From my original plan I measured the position of key landmarks, such as the lane and cottages. A layer of runny Polyfilla mixed with black powder paint was laid with the help of a

$\frac{1}{4}$ in paint brush, to form the lane. When this dried I used oil paints to give the surface a grey finish, working in a little yellow and brown in places. I decided that the meadow side of the land would be fenced while the Crabwood Cottage side would be bordered by hedges. Peco flexible fencing was used and, I think, proved quite successful. The length of field up to the old barn and the fence of Rose Cottage was covered with diluted Unibond and Peco Meadow Grass scattered on. I took care to leave an area of earth or mud around the gate where the cattle would tend to congregate when it came near to milking time!

Now I was ready to tackle the most important part of the scene, the cottages. These cottages were made in a style which I have found very pleasing in the past and simple to construct. The walls were cut from thick card with windows and doors carefully drawn in to harmonise with the contours. They were then cut out using a craft knife and a straight-edge. As the walls extend below the ground level, I found it useful to place a wall into the recess and mark a line across to show the level of the ground. The walls were strengthened with strips of $\frac{1}{8}$ in $\times$ $\frac{1}{2}$ in obeche and glued together, ensuring a fairly tight fit into the recess. I then removed the building from the landscape and applied a coat of Unibond to

Fig 1 *The cottage scene (drawing roughly to scale 52 cm × 70 cm).*

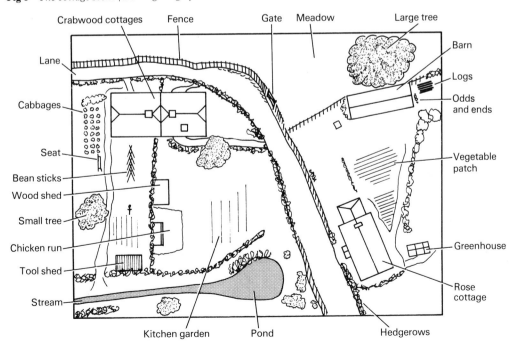

all walls and covered these with fine sand. When dry, the walls were painted with white undercoat and touched up in places with black paint on a dry brush. The window frames were made from thin card and glazed with whatever transparent material I had available, usually Plastiglaze. The doors were made from plastic card, carefully scribed with a craft knife and a straight-edge, with overlays of micro strip added to give a little relief. After painting, I added door handles, knockers and letter boxes with pieces of fuse wire and small off-cuts of plastic.

The roof areas were then covered with thick card and trimmed to size. The thatch effect was achieved by cutting lengths of thick wool and glueing across the card roof from eave to eave. When completed, the lengths were trimmed and glued under the eaves to give that overhang characteristic of the thatched roof. The whole roof area was covered with a diluted mix of Unibond which was worked into the wool layers with a small piece of obeche (an old $\frac{1}{4}$ in paint brush will do the job just as well) and then a fine brown scatter material was sprinkled on. On drying out thoroughly, the texture was then painted in oils using yellow and brown shades. Here the modeller can choose which colour to give the thatch; greys and browns are equally acceptable. The chimneys were made from balsa strips with computer punchings glued and painted red, to represent brickwork. The chimneys were glued into pre-cut holes in the roof.

All other buildings, including the barn, do not extend below the ground surface, the bottom edges being trimmed to match the contours. These were made largely from thin card cut into 'planks' and glued to a card framework and painted in a thin matt brown, working in some darker shades. The slate roof on the barn was made from individual pieces of Plastikard, glued in place and painted dark grey.

The back gardens were carefully marked out on the landscape, showing areas of footpath, shrubbery and vegetables. Let us look at Rose Cottage first. The area forms a trapezium shape, the widest part running from the lane and along the fence bordering the meadow. I decided to position the barn here as it would give a better balance to the overall landscape. The grassed area was marked out, diluted Unibond spread over the surface and Peco Meadow Grass scattered on. When dry, the surplus particles were gently brushed off and lichen bushes glued in place. The paths around the cottage and leading down to the barn were formed using fine sand glued to the surface and touched up with

greys and browns when dry. A slightly coarser scatter material was used to represent a gravel path. The small green borders around the foot of the cottage walls were made from strands of Woodland Scenes F53 (Dark Green), a truly excellent product. Other shades of green have been used elsewhere on the landscape. Small lichen bushes were then glued to the side of the cottage to form creeping shrubs. The rambling rose over the porch of the cottage was made from strands of Woodland Scenic dark green with touches of Humbrol 73, a mellow claret colour, to represent the roses. I found this method of representing flowers to be reasonably effective without being too time consuming. The flowers in the hedgerow stand out well if a liberal blob of paint is placed on the foliage material, particularly if it is white paint.

Now vegetables next! Lines of cabbages etc were laid out and once again, strands and small clumps of F53 provided the spinach and broccoli variety while John Piper Yellow Green Flock, LS6 glued into small balls with Evo-Stik and then flattened out, made very pleasing cabbages and were planted in rows. These types of vegetables appear in other gardens.

The steps leading into the adjoining outhouse were made from Peco Scene Texture Compound —surely one of the best modelling mediums ever invented. The compound was crudely glued into position and then carefully moulded with a knife and matchstick to form rough stone steps. The base of the greenhouse was also made using this compound, as were the flower pots inside! Small pieces of lichen were stuck into the painted compound and little blobs of red added to achieve a successful crop of tomato plants. The greenhouse was made from thin transparent plastic involving much toil in careful glueing and painting. Thank goodness Wills have put a kit on the market which will make this type of scenic accessory much easier to tackle! Twigs from the garden were cut and stacked around and inside the barn. Oddments of rustic life such as a cartwheel and chunks of old timber were stacked up against the far side of the barn—out of sight from the cottage! A small rabbit hutch was added and completed the back garden scene of Rose Cottage.

I then tackled Crabwood Cottage, which is in fact a double cottage but built as one unit, and the back gardens. The cottage was made in identical fashion to Rose Cottage with a small window added in one of the roofs. There is a little more detail inside the cottage such as a table lamp, a table and vase of beautiful roses, all of which are visible through the windows. As

2 *The front gate of Crabwood cottages. Note the sunflower to the right of the gate and the realistic flowering hedge. The rough texture of the cottage wall is also visible.*

3 *An end view of Crabwood cottages showing the back gardens. Mr McGregor is admiring his runner beans whilst Mrs McGregor is sitting on the garden seat.*

4 *The chicken run with the wood shed behind. Note the bicycle in the wood shed, the chopping block complete with axe and the scarecrow in the left upper corner of the photograph.*

the drawing shows, hedges border the lane from Crabwood Cottage to the pond and I set to work making sections of privet hedge to run between the front gates of the two cottages. For this I cut lengths of ordinary draught excluder. This is an ideal material as it is flexible and can be glued to the contour of the land. I covered the draught excluder with diluted Unibond and scattered Hammant & Morgan Dark Brown Foliage, carefully shaking off the surplus over a sheet of paper and using Evo-Stik on the bottom of the tape to glue the hedge in position. This gives a really pleasing appearance and when dry the hedge is quite rigid.

The steps leading up to the front doors of the cottage were made from Peco Texture Compound, as were the stone gate posts. The plants and shrubs around the cottage were made from lichen, Hammant & Morgan Foliage, scatter materials and John Piper scenic accessories. I did allow myself one extravagance —a sunflower, which was big enough to allow individual modelling attention. A small circular piece of card was glued on to a thin piece of

plastic rod, lichen and foliage added to the stem and the head painted in poster shades of yellow and brown. The flowers in the hedgerows were added by using the blob of white enamel paint method. When marking out the back gardens, I allowed for a thick hedge to border the stream and pond, with another hedge dividing the two plots. For this type of hedge I used John Piper Rubberised Horsehair cut in long strands, teased and painted in greens, yellows and browns before gluing down with Evo-Stik. The creeping ivy at the end of the cottage was made from dark green foliage glued on with Unibond.

The larger garden was laid out with a small lawn surrounded by shrubs and a path bordered by white stones (Peco Compound again) leading to the side entrance. To add interest to the remainder of the plot, I included a chicken run, with an old corrugated iron fence and a wood shed. Small twigs from my garden were cut and glued to form stacks of small logs and positioned in and around the shed. An axe can be seen resting in the chopping block while the cottage owner goes to greet the postman. The sacks near the chicken run were very effectively made from Peco Texture Compound. If the compound is rolled out into a big thin sausage and then cut at lengths of say, ¼ in, dozens of little sacks are formed complete with ears!

For those who have read *The Tales of Beatrix Potter*, the neighbouring garden has a special appeal, for it belongs to none other than Mr McGregor! He can be seen surveying the progress of his runner beans and lettuces. The wooden tool shed at the bottom of the garden has a corrugated roof. Logs are stacked in piles in the garden and spare canes can be seen standing against the shed. The old scarecrow surveys the rows of lettuces (Hammant & Morgan Light Green Foliage) and a pitch fork stands in the soil nearby. Behind Mr McGregor on the garden seat is his wife with the knitting by her side and stalking behind the bush is a rabbit—could it be Peter or maybe it is the one who likes eating cabbages!

The stream and pond were left virtually to the last item as this involved using clear varnish. The bed of the stream was given liberal coatings of brown and green enamel paint to ensure a

sealed, watertight surface. Shrubs, reeds and other greenery were glued to the edge of the stream and pond area. I then found a secure, level surface on which I placed the landscape and carefully poured the first layer of clear varnish into the stream. After a while the liquid found its own level and trickled into the pond and was allowed to dry. Successive layers were then added to arrive at the required level. A bubble formed between two such sessions but eventually disappeared—to my great relief. Some ducks then came on the scene, made by Dart Castings (as are the rabbits) and I have noticed many more scale animals and birds apppearing on the market to give life to the layout. A mother and daughter feeding the ducks made another little focus of interest on the landscape.

The last scenic items to be added were trees. Without doubt the more trees one has the greater appeal the layout offers. However, I have found trees the most difficult scenic item to master because Mother Nature still holds the upper hand! There are a number of ways one can tackle tree modelling and I eventually settled

5   *Rose cottage with its realistic thatched roof and a rambling rose around the door.*

6   *The barn at Rose cottage. Note the realistic wood planking and the roof in need of repairs.*

7   *A closer view of one end of the barn showing some of the many small details included in the scene.*

8   *The scratch-built greenhouse complete with plants and garden tools inside.*

for the multi-strand cable method. This time I visited my local motorcycle spares shop and purchased a length of cable. I cut the cable into lengths of between 5 cm and 15 cm depending on the height of the tree. One end was then twisted out with the aid of pliers and the main cables separated down as far as halfway. Each one of these was then further twisted and shaped to form a main branch and its off-shoots. I found that four or five such lengths, when held together, shaped up into quite a reasonable looking tree. The straight lengths forming the trunk were bound together with thin wire and a piece of wire or nail was inserted into the bottom of the trunk to form a locating pin. The cable was then soldered to form a trunk. DAS modelling clay was used to represent the bark and was carefully glued around the trunk with Evo-Stik and stippled with a dry brush to give a rough surface. The clay hardens fairly quickly if left in a dry, well ventilated place. After this, and subsequent operations, I found it helpful to stand the tree on a piece of wood with a hole drilled to accept the locating pin. For areas of trunk and branch which tend to be inaccessible to the hand, the clay can be moistened and applied with a brush, building up successive layers if necessary.

Painting the branches and trunk requires care in selecting suitable colours. It is difficult to paint a skeleton tree with a brush as the branches must be given individual attention. A good way of overcoming this is to spray the tree with, say, a dark grey or brown matt paint. The trunk and larger branches can then be given a more realistic finish by adding artists' oils for greys

greens and yellows and finishing with a coat of matt varnish for added protection.

That was the easy bit! Now for the foliage. I originally used the John Piper Rubberised Fibre, cut into small clumps, teased a little to thin them out and then glued these to the branches, making sure that the tree developed balanced proportions. Diluted Unibond was then painted on to these clumps and Hammant & Morgan Woodland Scenics Dark Green Foliage particles were scattered on giving the effect shown in the illustrations. I found that perhaps the tree looked a little too 'full' and so I made some birch trees using only the Hammant & Morgan Foliage teased out to give the feathery effect of leaves. The finished trees were then planted in the landscape. Trees require very careful study before modelling because each has its own characteristics and charm, and different species can be represented with a little practice. All that remains to complete the scene is the village postman on his rounds, the local carrier on his weekly delivery of perishables and a few cows grazing in the meadow.

I have tended to refer to the model as a landscape because, like an artist, I feel that I have created my own little corner of the English countryside as it was seen perhaps half a century ago. Scenic modelling is a three dimensional art and plays the vital role of knitting the whole model railway layout together. Even on a small layout, there is tremendous potential for scenic modelling and a few visits to exhibitions will quickly prove the point. However, it would appear that I was so engrossed in my landscape detail that I totally overlooked the railway! ●

Model a harbour

Michael Andress

The first harbour on a model railway layout that I can recall seeing was Madderport, on John Ahern's famous Madder Valley Railway. It was featured in a children's book published in the 1940s in which the story was illustrated with full colour photographs of model railways. More than 30 years later this attractive book is still in my library, and the Madder Valley Railway is still in existence, on display at Pendon Museum. Another well known layout that featured a harbour, Ron Bryant's pioneer 000-gauge Inversnecky & Drambuie branch of the Highland Railway, has also, I believe, passed to a museum, the Railway Museum at York.

Since these layouts were built other expert scenic modellers have also included harbours or docks on their layouts to very good effect. There are many advantages both scenically and operationally in featuring a small port on your model railway. The water, the dock or wharf, the ships and boats, the cranes and structures, and the many smaller details are all very interesting in model form. For the real railways, links with shipping at docks, harbours and canals have always been of great importance and, similarly, on a model railway such a facility will provide much additional freight traffic, both in amount and in its variety.

You may feel that because you have space for only a small layout then you could not include a dock or harbour as there would not be room for it. However, by choosing a suitable prototype, always the key to successful modelling of any sort, we can model such a scene very realistically, even in 00 gauge, on a small layout. Obviously the large port with its ocean-going passenger liners, massive container ships and huge super-tankers is out of the question, but this would be unsuitable anyway because, even if we had enough space, the rest of the layout would be dwarfed by the port. In fact, there are many small docks around the country, often with only a single wharf, serving coastal steamers, which would be ideal for modelling. I have included a photograph of just such a dock which though small and simple has facilities for handling sand, gravel and coal. As it happens this wharf is served by road vehicles and not by rail but in model form one or two sidings could easily be provided. Most layouts could accommodate a model based on this prototype and the scenic possibilities and the additional traffic and shunting generated would more than compensate for the area it would occupy. In N gauge it may well be possible to build something rather more elaborate without using too much space. An example is the model dock, oil depot and ship building yard built by Graham Bailey to fit within the loop at one end of his 'dog-bone' shaped N-gauge layout. The model is shown in one of the accompanying photographs.

1 *Madderport station and harbour on John Ahern's well-known Madder Valley Railway, now on display at the Pendon Museum. Note the light at the harbour entrance and the realistic effect achieved at the rear of the layout with the low relief structures and scenic background (Pendon Museum).*

2 *Graham Bailey modelled this busy dock area for his N-gauge layout. The ship is the Novo 'Shell Welder' kit, the cranes were built from Pola kits and the oil tanks are from the Faller range. The water was modelled with fibreglass resin.*

3 *This small wharf would be an ideal basis for a model. Note the typical construction of the wooden wharf side and the small coastal vessel.*

You may argue that your layout has to be very small and that you really cannot afford space for a harbour. In fact, I would suggest the converse, that the less space you have the more seriously you should consider a dock! As I will show later a harbour can be suggested in an absolute minimum of area, and it will provide a greater variety of traffic and scenic possibilities than almost anything else. Thus a dock will add to the operating potential and make your small layout more interesting to run so that you will be less likely to tire of running it. The scope for scenic detailing is also considerable and you will find that you can spend many happy hours of modelling, adding small details to the harbour area, thus adding to the constructional interest of your layout. Much of the pleasure in railway modelling comes from the construction work and the more there is of this the longer the layout will hold the interest of the modeller.

As in any type of modelling, reference to the real thing is invaluable in helping you to achieve a realistic result. If you would like to build a harbour or dock for your layout I would certainly recommend that you take every opportunity to visit prototype docks to get ideas and information. It is most convenient to take a camera with you so that you can take pictures of anything of interest for future reference, though failing this you can make notes and sketches to help you later. Remember that even if a particular structure or other feature would be too large to be modelled exactly you can always use part of it, or just details from it, for your own models. You will find that there is a considerable variety in size and type of docks, including, for example, small fishing harbours, a single wharf handling just one local product, a car ferry terminal, a port and industrial area with a variety of different factories and installations, and so on. Try to choose features which are appropriate and typical for the sort of

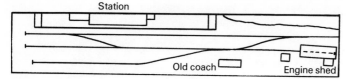

Fig 1   *An example of a minimum space branch line terminus design.*

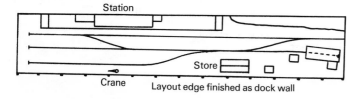

Fig 2   *By finishing the front edge of the baseboard as a harbour wall, and adding a few details such as a hand crane, the siding can serve the dock, adding interest scenically and operationally without requiring any additional space.*

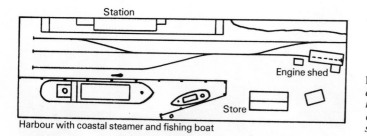

Fig 3   *If additional space is available the model can be made even more interesting by including part of the harbour with one or more ships.*

dock you are modelling as this will create the most realistic effect.

I would now like to consider some of the ways in which a harbour or dock can be fitted into a typical layout design. As I hinted above, in the extreme case of space restrictions we can include a dock with virtually no increase in layout size. If, for example, we take the typical branch line terminus, as shown above, it is easy to suggest the presence of a dock. If we merely finish the baseboard edge as a dock wall, set the adjacent track into the ground and provide a small crane, we can create the impression of a harbour with its own siding. Many further details can be added to improve the effect and we should also choose railway and other structures of an architectural type appropriate to the coastal area in which we want to set our model. Here there is plenty of scope, from Scotland to Cornwall! This arrangement is the bare minimum and obviously the effect will be even better if we can spare a few extra inches at the front to model the water surface together with one or more ships or boats. An alternative is to model the dock at the rear of the layout behind the terminus station, again served by a siding or sidings, which can be in front of or behind the dock.

On an oval track scheme layout a harbour can be featured within the oval of track providing not only an interesting scenic feature and extra traffic but also serving to separate visually the two sides of the oval making the layout seem larger and more realistic. An interesting variant on this idea is to build a continuous run layout with a central operating well. This is finished off with a dock wall all round and the well represents the dock itself. A number of sidings can be provided on the oval to serve the dock, warehouses, an oil depot, other industries, and so on. Such a layout will give great scope for operation, especially if one of the card order systems is used to determine the distribution of the goods rolling stock. There will also be excellent possibilities for building detailed industrial structures of various types, keeping the modeller happily busy for a considerable time! If you already have an oval layout built you may be able to fit a small extension on to it, perhaps at the site at which a siding leads from the oval, to provide space for a small dock. If necessary this could be a removable section which is fitted on to the layout only for operating sessions.

Having considered some of the arrangements we can employ to include a dock we can now look more closely at some of the details of construction. Harbour or dock walls are usually either of stone blocks or wooden construction. For a stone wall we can use any of the usual methods of modelling. One of the simplest is to mount commercial printed stone paper on to a support of card or sheet wood. The Faller printed card material has the advantage of being embossed giving a more realistic appearance. An alternative is to use embossed stone course plastic card. This is thin styrene sheet and will also require mounting on a support; thicker plastic card or sheet wood will be suitable. The embossed plastic card will need to be painted but the resulting surface is very realistic. For those who like a more individual touch, stone courses can be scribed into a coating of plaster, Peco Texture Modelling Compound, or Pyruma (or Kos) fire cement. This job could be speeded up by using a stone press of the type devised by Allan Downes and described in his article on wall modelling. Another method would be to build up the length of wall from Linka castings which give a very realistic representation of stone work. Alternatively, the modeller could cast the wall in plaster (dental plaster as available from Boots chemists is ideal) or in Linkalite Casting Compound using a mould he has constructed himself.

Often stone harbour walls have timbers on them and these can be modelled from stripwood, either balsa or hardwood, cut to length and glued in place. Stone steps can be built up from plastic card or from Peco Texture Modelling Compound or Pyruma, depending on the material you have employed for the wall itself. Further details include iron mooring rings (from wire), old rubber tyres used as bumpers or fenders to avoid damage to vessel sides (military vehicle kits are a useful source) and bollards along the top (easily fabricated from dowel and scraps of wire or plastic).

Wooden dock walls, together with any jetties, landing stages and wharves of wooden construction can be built up from stripwood or dowelling for the piles, stripwood for the longitudinal beams and bracing strips, and scribed sheet wood for the walls and decks. A good weathered wood effect can be achieved with a wash of diluted mixed black and brown model paint. This is best applied to the wood before assembly as this stain will not soak into the wood wherever there is glue on the surface. For the most realistic results I would recommend that you copy from one or more real docks when modelling these features. There are many suitable prototypes around the country, with considerable variations between them, so I am sure that you will find something appropriate for your model without difficulty. A few photographs will be invaluable in refreshing your memory when you come to work on your layout.

In the industrial and dock areas the railway tracks are often inset so that vehicles and workmen can cross them easily and safely. This can be copied in model form by building up the ground surface to the height of the rail tops, and will add greatly to the appearances. A simple method is to use card, butting it against the outer sides of the rails; a strip is also fitted between the rails making sure that there is sufficient clearance. The card can be surfaced with printed stone paper or, even better, with the flexible paved street material from Preiser or the cobblestone foil from Vollmer, or can simply be painted grey to represent tarmac. Another method is to use plaster which can then be scribed to reproduce the appearance of setts or cobblestones though this is a tedious technique to employ for more than a small area. As with the card, care must be taken to leave adequate clearance for the wheels of the locomotives and rolling stock. Probably the simplest and easiest method of producing a realistic effect is to use the moulded plastic cobblestone sheet produced by the Loughborough Model Shop. This is designed for use with 00-gauge tramway models but is equally suitable for inset railway tracks. Straight and curved sections are available and include pieces to be placed outside and between the rails. They are suitable for use with all the main brands of ready-made track available.

To form the water in the dock or harbour we can use any of the various techniques which have been devised for scenic modelling. For some of these the dock wall should be in place before the water is modelled, with others it will be added afterwards. One of the simplest methods, if the water in the dock is to be still and without ripples or waves, is to use a piece of hardboard, smooth side up, as the water surface. This is painted appropriately in blue-green, brown or even black depending on the effect desired. When the paint has dried the surface is given several coats of clear gloss varnish to give a wet look to the modelled water. An alternative to varnishing is to place a sheet of ripple glass on top of the painted hardboard. This gives a very realistic effect but has the disadvantage that the glass is relatively heavy, particularly if there is a large area of water to be modelled. Also care must be taken not to drop anything on to the glass in case it cracks or

4

5

6

7

8

4 Michael Walshaw fitted this small dock between two sidings at the rear of the terminus station on his Westport Branch. The tracks have been realistically inset. For more pictures of this interesting layout see the article beginning on page 4.

5 A small fishing port, beautifully modelled by Dave Rowe for his 4 mm scale narrow-gauge layout. The harbour wall and steps, as well as the structures, were made from Peco Texture Modelling Compound. The fishing boats were scratch-built. Homekraft rough texture modelling clay, carefully shaped to form the waves, was employed for the realistic sea. This was painted and, while still wet, the white foam of the waves was blended in. Several coats of clear gloss varnish completed the effect (Peco).

6 Inset track on a small wharf in 00 gauge. Extra rails were fitted between the running rails to provide clearance for the wheels. Plaster was then applied and carved when dry to represent the stones.

7 Repairs and repainting of smaller ships and boats is often carried out with the vessel lifted from the water without the need for a dry dock, as with this tug in Gothenburg. Note also the old rubber tyres hung on the stone wall to act as fenders.

8 P. D. Hancock modelled a rather similar scene for a boat building and repair yard at Craig on his famous Craig & Mertonford Railway layout. Note the many realistic small details included in this scene (P.D. Hancock).

9 This Scottish village and harbour makes a very attractive scenic feature on Ron Bryant's TT-gauge North Caledonian Railway layout. The fishing trawler is a Pyro kit for a modern diesel trawler which has been backdated by fitting a scratch-built wheel-house and funnel, while the tug is a modified Revell kit (John Roxburgh).

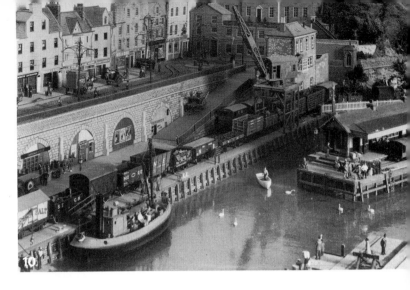

10 *Craig Harbour on P.D. Hancock's narrow-gauge Craig & Mertonford Railway layout. In addition to the narrow-gauge line there are also standard-gauge tracks and a tramway, as can be seen in this picture. Note the many small details which this expert scenic modeller has included in the scene. The water is ripple glass* (P.D. Hancock).

shatters, and this fragility can also be a problem for a portable layout. Rather than place the glass directly on to the painted surface, some modellers like to leave a gap, of perhaps an inch or so, giving a greater impression of depth to the water. Weeds, rocks, even a sunken rowing boat, can be placed on the bottom and will appear to be submerged in the water. If you are modelling a jetty you will need to cut the pilings so that the underwater sections can be mounted beneath the glass and the above water parts on top of the glass water surface.

Another method for representing water is to model the surface in plaster or other similar material. This is then painted and later given several coats of clear gloss varnish. The surface can be modelled flat for a dead calm stretch of water, gently rippled or with waves as desired. One of the accompanying photographs shows Llareggub Harbour on Dave Rowe's well known 'Milk Wood' 4 mm scale narrow-gauge layout. The very realistic sea, complete with waves, was made from modelling clay painted and varnished.

A very effective technique which has become popular recently is the use of clear casting plastic to model water on model railway layouts, and indeed for military and other model dioramas. This material is available from craft and toy shops and is supplied as liquid plastic and hardener which are mixed just before use. The plastic is poured on to the harbour or dock bed in layers and when it has set hard it gives a very realistic effect. The surface can be given a rippled appearance either by mixing a larger amount of hardener into the final layer or by using a hair dryer to blow hot air across the surface as it sets. An alternative but cheaper material which gives similar results is fibreglass resin and this was employed by Graham Bailey

to form the water in the harbour scene shown in one of the accompanying pictures.

The structures required for the dock area will depend on the size and type of facility that you are modelling. In the simplest form you may only need one or two sheds or small storage buildings. The typical dockside warehouses are interesting structures and can often be modelled in low relief along the rear of the layout, behind the harbour. The Bilteezi range of card kits includes one for an attractive stone-built warehouse of traditional design and the series of plans by John Ahern, available from MAP, also features a warehouse of this type. There are many other structures which can be situated by the dock. The plastic kits produced by the various Continental manufacturers include many suitable items, such as the gravel works and cement works from Faller, the gravel silo, cement towers and cement hoppers, and the oil storage tanks and other oil depot facilities from Kibri, and the oil refinery units from Vollmer. Even greater variety is possible from scratch-building. Dockside cranes are available as plastic kits from Airfix and Pola; for a smaller dock a hand crane may be appropriate and one of the goods yard cranes from the Mike's Models cast metal kit series would be ideal.

Obviously the appearance of our model dock or harbour will be further enhanced by the provision of suitable ships or boats adding scenic interest. Many railway modellers are not aware of what is avilable in this respect and may end up either omitting vessels entirely or using inappropriate or out of scale toys. This is a pity because, although the range of suitable models on the market is rather limited, there are enough for the railway modeller to create a good effect on his layout. Wiad did make a tug, also available with a canopy as a river boat, intended for

HO scale and these ready-made models are now available from Noch. They are fully finished but are rather expensive. Though a little underscale for 00 they are acceptable; they could also be employed on a TT-scale layout. The Revell American Harbour tug, a plastic kit model, scales out at just under 3 mm to the foot making it perfect for TT, but it is also acceptable for 00 and HO scales. It lends itself well to modifications and Ron Bryant has made changes to the model so that it appears less modern for use on his Scottish prototype TT-gauge layout. He has also back-dated the modern fishing trawler kit made by Pyro by fitting a new funnel and wheelhouse and the completed model can be seen in Tapwater Harbour in the accompanying picture. There are several other American plastic ship model kits which can be used, if necessary with alterations, but their availability in this country varies so I would suggest you have a browse in your local model shop. The Airfix Great Western paddle steamer is approximately N scale but can be used as the basis for an 00-scale model of a smaller prototype. I have successfully converted it into a paddle tug and it should also be possible to make a small passenger paddle steamer for 00 scale from it.

For the modeller prepared to scratch-build ship models for his layout, the Skinley 4 mm scale waterline ship model plans are ideal as the prototypes have been selected especially for model railway layouts. They range from a steel hopper barge (8 inches long) to the LNER Harwich Train Ferry (53 inches long) and there is a total of 23 different models. By halving all dimensions the plans can be used for N-gauge layouts. In fact, if you have any structure or rolling stock modelling experience using wood, card or plastic card you should be able to construct these ship models very successfully and I would certainly recommend trying one of the plans, perhaps for one of the smaller and simpler models first of all.

Several small boats are commercially available. Preiser include a set of three rowing boats complete with boatmen and oars in their range of ready painted figures and accessories. Noch make canoes with paddles, a motor cruiser, a sailing cruiser and a sailing catamaran. The Lesney and Wiking ranges both include a motor boat and trailer; the Wiking model is complete with a realistic outboard motor. These motor boats can be removed from the trailers and used separately if desired. The lifeboats from plastic ship kits, such as those made by Airfix and Revell, are useful as small boats for model harbours. They are usually to a smaller scale

than 00, but removing some of the seats give realistic rowing boats for this scale and masts and booms of thin strip wood and sails of paper can easily be added to make small sailing boats. Rowing and sailing dinghies, canoes, punts and so on can also be modelled quite simply from scratch using wood, card and paper.

For N-gauge layouts the Revell Kandahar Fishing Trawler and the Novo Shell Welder tanker appear to be suitable. Graham Bailey has used the latter kit very effectively on his layout, both as a fully completed model and partly assembled to represent a ship under construction in his model ship building yard. As I mentioned above the Airfix Great Western is approximately N scale; it could be converted to the other types of paddle steamers as required. A motor barge, available either as an open barge or as an oil tanker version, suitable for N scale, was made by Wiad. It may still be on the market, either from Wiad or from Noch.

There are innumerable small details which can be included and which will add to the interest and appeal of a dock or harbour scene. Careful study of the picture of P. D. Hancock's beautifully detailed Craig Harbour will indicate the possibilities. If you can I would also suggest that you go and look at some real harbours and docks to get further ideas. These small details not only make the model more interesting but if appropriately chosen will help to give the right atmosphere to the scene. We are fortunate nowadays, particularly for 00 and HO layouts, in the very wide range of scenic detail accessories available either as plastic or cast metal kits or ready-made models. There is a fine selection of human and animal figures of all types and poses, many of them exquisitely detailed, and including even small items such as swans and seagulls! We can also obtain packing cases, barrels, oil drums, crates, trunks, suitcases, packages, dustbins, sacks, carboys, trolleys, small trucks, wheelbarrows, bicycles, motor-cycles, and so on. Some excellent road vehicle kits, mainly of cast metal type, are also produced so that we can include accurately modelled lorries and vans in the dock area. It is also easy to model many other items from scraps of wood, card, plastic and wire and a great deal of enjoyment can be obtained from adding realistic details in this way.

To close I hope that I have been able to convince you that a dock or harbour would be a worthwhile addition to your layout and that you will gain as much pleasure as I have from this aspect of railway modelling. ●

Scenic backgrounds

Michael Andress

When making the scenery for a railway layout most modellers construct and colour the three dimensional landscape first of all. They then select a suitable scenic background and erect this along the rear edge of the layout. The addition of such a backscene is a worthy idea but, to achieve the greatest benefit from this feature, we really need to do some pre-planning rather than merely considering it as an afterthought. In this article I would like to make some suggestions about using scenic backgrounds more effectively and realistically. You may not agree with all, or indeed with any, of these ideas but if I can provoke at least some thought about how you employ backscenes on your layout then I will be well satisfied!

These backgrounds are an important part of the scenic work on a model railway layout and can improve its appearance in several ways. They eliminate from view distracting features such as furniture, patterned wallpaper and curtains, and so on behind the layout, so that your attention is held better by the models. This is also very noticeable in photographs where even a plain white background is a great improvement. A scenic background can also be used to complete the scene and to give an impression of depth and distance which can add greatly to the realism and effectiveness of the layout. These backgrounds are very useful for concealing a fiddle yard or other hidden tracks or sidings, providing a complete scenic break between the visible and concealed tracks in a minimum of depth. Backscenes are usually thought of in terms of placement along the rear of an all along the wall, or around the wall, type of layout, rather than for an island layout design such as, for example, the typical train set oval and its developments. Obviously it is not feasible to place a backscene all the way round the periphery of an island layout unless it is operated from a central well and, in this latter case, it is really a form of around the wall layout in effect. Backscenes can, though, be employed very effectively on an island layout along one or two sides or as a central divider, providing a scenic break between the two sides of the layout.

Such a divider can be a double-sided backscene providing a background for each side of the layout. This scheme helps to conceal the round and round nature of such an oval track design and adds to the realism both scenically and operationally by creating the impression of two separate areas between which the trains run. This central divider can be placed only within the oval or, on a layout for two operators, can be extended further, to divide the layout into two completely separate sides.

Experienced modellers often draw and paint their own background scenes to match their scenery. Many of these are very effective and realistic and they are, of course, 'tailor made' for the situation. However, there can be difficulties, particularly with perspective and colour, and the majority of modellers choose to rely on the commercially produced backscenes. As with most things there are advantages and disadvantages to this choice. In their favour is the fact that they have been specially designed for this purpose so that the choice of subject, the scale and the colouring are appropriate. Often the artists have drawn them in perspective in such a way that they are realistic from a reasonable range of viewpoints rather than from just one position. Most are printed in full colour from artists' drawings except for the Faller and Vollmer sheets which appear to be reproductions of colour photographs, and the Skinley sheets which are line drawings for the modeller himself to colour as he wishes. The scenes are usually designed so that the different sheets of the set made by any one manufacturer will fit together in any order with the joins matching. It may also be possible to combine sheets or parts of sheets from different makers successfully, if necessary using trees, buildings, or other features to conceal the joins, though variation in styles and colours may cause problems.

Quite a wide variety of scenes are available from manufacturers in Britain, the United States and Germany. Naturally the scenes produced in Britain are the most appropriate for layouts set in this country, though some of the other back-

1, 2 *These two pictures show the same model scene from the identical viewpoint but, for the second photograph, a printed scenic background has been placed behind the models; the improvement in appearance and realism is self evident! The background is an American product made originally by HO West and now available from Walthers.*

3 *Two British scenic backgrounds. Above is an attractive seascape from the VA Bilteezi range marketed by Hamblings. The Peco sheet below is designed to be cut out and either mounted on to other sheets or used as 'flats' in front of another scenic background.*

4, 5 *Two views of Owlburn station on Ian Anderson's 00-gauge Owlburn & Mousehill layout. The realistic scenic background was produced by mounting features cut from Bilteezi sheets on to Peco backgrounds. The low relief structures are converted Builder Plus kits. Note how the wall has been used to mask the junction of modelled and printed scenery* (Malcolm Noyce).

grounds are also suitable. Obviously the type of rural or urban scene must match up as far as possible with the modelled scenery and buildings on the layout. Usually a suitable backscene can be found but this is a limitation of the commercially produced backgrounds. Another disadvantage is that they are frequently seen on other layouts so that we lose some individuality. However, despite these possible drawbacks, the commercial backscenes have much to commend them. They are generally well designed and produced, they are not expensive, and they make it easy for the modeller to complete the scenery on his layout.

Because they can be so easy and quick to erect it is tempting to think of them as a form of instant background scenery which requies little effort on our part. However, with a little more thought and work we can minimise the disadvantages mentioned above and get the most realistic results possible from these backscenes. In the remainder of this article I would like to make some suggestions on how you can use the commercially produced backgrounds most effectively on your layout.

As I have already implied there is a tendency to add a backscene as the last touch after the rest of the scenery has been completed. While you may be able to get away with this if you make your own scenic background, drawn and painted to suit the situation, the addition of one of the commercial backgrounds in this way is much less likely to be successful. Too often the match between modelled and printed scenery will be poor and the scenic background looks like an afterthought. Obviously we will choose

as comparable a scene as possible, be it a landscape or a village, town or city view, but for the best results we must consider which scenic background sheets we will use at the time when we first plan the scenery. It is essential to think of the modelled scenery and the background together as an entity. Indeed I would even venture to suggest that the best blending of the two, using a commercial background, may come from making the selection of suitable backscenes the first step in planning and modelling the scenery. The background could be erected first, providing something in the way of a scenic setting for the railway, before the modelled scenery is built. Then, as time permits, the three dimensional scenery can be modelled using the printed scenery of the background as a guide for the contours and the colours of the scenery. I realise this idea is a controversial one but it has much to recommend it and is certainly worthy of consideration! Even if you are not prepared to go as far as adopting this scheme it is desirable to have decided on the backscene you will use before modelling the scenery which will lie in front of it.

A criticism of the commercial scenes is that they are so frequently seen on layouts that they are instantly recognisable for what they are and so lose some of their effectiveness. One method to disguise this 'sameness' is to mount sections cut from one scenic background sheet on to another. For example, a house, tree or hill cut from one scene can be mounted on another sheet, covering part of it and giving it a different appearance. In some cases the manufacturer has made provision for this type of approach. One of the Peco sheets consists of features specifically intended for cutting out and mounting on other sheets in the series to provide extra variety. The Townscene backgrounds produced by Brian Sherriff Ltd also include many separate and complete buildings to be cut out and assembled in any order or combination,

making this series very versatile indeed. Rather than include a sky background on the individual sheets of this series, which would lead to difficulties in concealing the joins, this firm also markets sky backgrounds 11 yards long. From such a roll the modeller can cut the length needed in one piece without joins. The various buildings can be mounted on this as required. In addition to the sheets designed by the manufacturers to be used like this there is, of course, nothing to stop you treating the ordinary sheets in the same way, giving even greater scope for variation. The sheets may be from the same series or can even be from different makers.

Even more effective than mounting these additional features directly on to the backscene is to use them as 'flats' or cut-outs, as is done with stage scenery in theatres. In this case the cut-out features are mounted on thick card, braced on the rear surface if necessary to prevent warping, and are then positioned a centimetre or two in front of the background. If desired there can even be two or three rows of these 'flats', each row slightly separated from the one behind. This separation gives an excellent effect of depth, enhanced by the fact that they change position in relation to the background with changes in the position of the viewer. The card should be sanded thinner at the edges and is best painted matt black on the rear while the edges should be touched up with paint to match up with the printed scene. The appearance of these 'flats' can be made even better by adding a little relief or texture to them. For example, on a 'flat' showing a small hill, patches of lichen can be glued to represent bushes. Building 'flats' lend themselves very well to the addition of a little relief. Window sills, doorsteps, drain pipes, door knobs, and many other small details can easily be fitted. Windows can be cut out and clear plastic glazing added; black card fitted behind these windows will prevent the viewer from realising that there is no depth to the

6 *A combination of low relief structures from the Superquick range of card kits, cut-outs made from Hamblings Bilteezi scenic backgrounds and a simple painted backscene gives a realistic impression of depth behind Westport station on Mike Walshaw's 00-gauge layout. This layout is described and illustrated in full in another article.*

7 *A scene on Ron Bryant's extensive TT-gauge layout, based on the North Caledonian Railway. The blending of the Peco scenic background and the modelled scenery in front of it has been skilfully achieved. The junction is just behind the fence. (John Roxburgh).*

8 *If a modelled road or river passes back towards the scenic background it is best to arrange the scenery so that the actual junction with the backscene is concealed as it is difficult to model this join realistically. On this Peco N-gauge exhibition layout the road curves round to the right behind a low hill so that its junction with the scenic background is concealed. The effect is realistic and natural. Note also how well the blending between the foreground scenery and the Peco scenic background has been carried out* (Peco).

9 *Ian Anderson's 00-gauge Owlburn & Mousehill layout, with the builder and his son at the controls. The scenic background has been mounted around the central operating well to give a neat and realistic appearance to the layout. Note also the double-sided extension of the scenic background at the right-hand end of the layout. This provides a visual separation between the two stations and adds greatly to the effect. Good use has also been made of low relief structures* (Malcolm Noyce).

structure.

In the same way modelled features, either full or low relief, placed in front of the scenic background will obscure parts of it, making it less recognisable. A rather effective method with a country scene where there are low hills on the background is to frame part of the backscene with small hills, modelled in low relief, at each side so that we appear to be looking into the distance through the gap between the hills. For a

town a combination of low relief structures, building 'flats' and a printed scenic background can be very realistic indeed if carefully arranged.

One of the most important points in the use of scenic backgrounds is the treatment of the junction between the three dimensional modelled scenery and the printed backscene. We want these to blend imperceptibly so we need to disguise or conceal the actual junction. There are two different basic methods of dealing with this problem. The usual technique is to mask the junction with modelled features, either in full or low relief, such as trees and bushes, fences and walls, low hills, an embankment or buildings. If the space is available it is best to leave a gap of perhaps 1 or 2 centimetres between the modelled and printed scenery to give a greater effect of depth. Then, for example, at the rear of the layout we may have a grassy bank with a fence or hedge along the top. The back of this bank drops straight down, in front of the background. Thus the junction is realistically concealed. It is important to arrange the lighting of the layout so that there are no shadows on the scenic background from trees, buildings or other modelled features as this immediately spoils the effect of a distant scene. The 'flats' I mentioned above can also be employed very successfully to conceal the junction area from view. If there is room the use of two or three rows of these 'flats' with a little gap between each row is particularly good.

The alternative method of handling the junction is rather more difficult but can be very realistic. In this case the modelled scenery is carried right up to the scenic background. This is most applicable for mountainous scenery, the plaster being brought right up and just on to the background. The modelled scenery is then painted to match the colours of the printed scene being used. Trees and bushes can be a mixture of fully modelled ones, some that are partly modelled and are stuck on to the background, and the ones already on the printed scene or added to it by being painted on. By using smaller and smaller modelled trees as we go further back towards the rear of the modelled scenery we can create forced perspective giving a greater feeling of depth and distance.

I mount my backgrounds on hardboard sheets, fixing them on to the smooth surface of the hardboard with wallpaper paste. To prevent any warping I brace the hardboard on its rear surface with strips of wood. The completed mounted backgrounds are fixed on to the layout with screws so that I can remove them when necessary for transportation or storage of the layout. Obviously if you decide to use the method in which the scenery is modelled up on to the background, the backscene would have to be fixed permanently on to the layout.

A rather effective treatment for a town or city backscene is to make small holes where the windows are in some of the buildings on the background and fit small lights behind the backscene so that these can be switched on for a very realistic night effect. It is also possible to illuminate building 'flats' by fitting small bulbs behind them, screened so that the light is only seen through the windows. ●

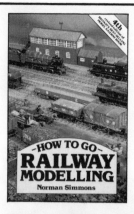